ROUTE 66
TRAVELER'S GUIDE AND ROADSIDE COMPANION

COLLECTOR'S EDITION

TOM SNYDER
FOUNDER AND DIRECTOR,
US ROUTE 66 ASSOCIATION

ST. MARTIN'S GRIFFIN ≈ NEW YORK

A NOTE TO THE READER

You will notice a few advertisements from the 1930s scattered throughout this guide. Although none of these businesses are to be found along the highway today, the ads provide something of the charm and allure of way-back-then travel over Route 66.

ROUTE 66 TRAVELER'S GUIDE AND ROADSIDE COMPANION—COLLECTOR'S EDITION. Copyright © 2000 by Thomas J. Snyder. All rights reserved. Printed in the United States of America. No part of this book may be used or reproduced in any manner whatsoever without written permission except in the case of brief quotations embodied in critical articles or reviews. For information address St. Martin's Press, 175 Fifth Avenue, New York, N.Y. 10010.

All strip maps appearing in this guide remain fully copyrighted by the Automobile Club of Southern California, and are reproduced here by special arrangement.

Cover: 1960 Corvette by Chevrolet, 1932 Roadster by Ford. Designed by the author.

Photo credits. Page 121: Chicago Skyline, 1946. US Route 66 Association Collection. *Page 125:* Chain of Rocks Bridge. James R. Powell Collection. *Page 131:* Brush Creek Bridge. US Route 66 Association Collection. *Page 134:* Robbers Road. US Route 66 Association Collection. *Page 139:* Midpoint Signs. US Route 66 Association Collection. *Page 143:* New Mexico House. US Route 66 Association Collection. *Page 155:* Rimmy Jim. Courtesy Janice Griffith, Pioneer Trails Museum. *Page 164:* Okie Family. Dorothea Lange, courtesy Library of Congress. *Page 176:* Santa Monica Pier. US Route 66 Association Collection.

ISBN 0-312-25417-2

10   9   8   7   6   5

DEDICATED TO

Charles Kuralt, whose wisdom and unerring sense of story set the standard for everyone with an urge to write about America's two-lane treasures. His reporting was unique to him, as was his plain, well-here-we-are style of writing. Charles taught decency and human value by example, and his CBS *Sunday Morning* show was a chalice, giving bright reflection to life on Route 66.

On the 4th of July in 1997, Charles Kuralt died and America is far poorer for his passing, though he would find that hard to imagine. Still, if there is a hereafter, Charles is already traveling it, sharing his discoveries of some back-country lane—a woman who cans heavenly peaches perhaps, or a man whose car will run for eternity on a single lump of coal.

Charles even knew how to make us feel better about being left behind. "Every road is as good as a promise and the promises all will be kept," he once said. "And do not worry about getting lost. I have gone on ahead and know the way."

ACKNOWLEDGMENTS

This collection was brought to life with the early support of Todd Appleman, and the generosity of travelers and roadsiders alike who opened their hearts to contribute these and other tales.

We are indebted to Delbert Benedict; Boyd Cabanis; Dixie Pryor Carter; Lester Clarkson; Curtis Coffey; Bruce Debo; Cari Gail; Bonnie Flowers; Mike Fry; Stephen and Glaida Funk; Janice Griffith; Joann Harwell; Dan Herrera; Fran Hauser; Susan Kirby; Dorothy Kvols; Linda Landini; Derik Lattig; Ellen Lawson; Anna Lee Lewis; Francis Maddox; Doris Katt McGill; Lynn Monkus; Cdr. Frank A. Munroe, USN (Ret.); Scott Nelson; Sally Noe; Margie Snowden North; Diane Patterson; The Tommy Pike Family; Mike Pitel; Jim Powell; Sandy Rosenberger; Steve Rossi and Mary Rossi Ott; Angel Shoemaker; Tom Smith; Don Wardlaw; Kathleen Winters; Martin Zanzuchhi, and others preferring no mention.

Of course, not all the stories found here warrant the label of Absolute Truth—one person's truth, even in pure science, is another's shaky ground. But it is a better history that makes room for both legends and laughter. So we leave it for you to decide. And to enjoy.

Finally a special thanks goes to the production crew at St. Martin's Press, and to my editor Julia Pastore, whose charm and enthusiasm transformed this task into a gladdening process.

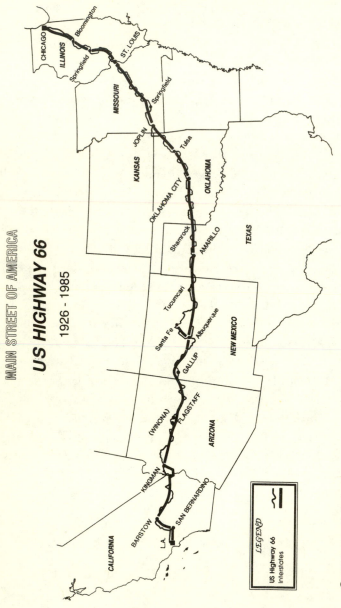

MAIN STREET OF AMERICA

US HIGHWAY 66

1926 - 1985

LEGEND

US Highway 66
Interstates

© US Route 66 Association

CONTENTS

AUTHOR'S NOTE

Like the road itself, this edition of the *Route 66 Traveler's Guide and Roadside Companion* embraces both happy and sad moments.

We're pleased to bring you the many revisions that reflect new friends and attractions found along the highway, plus dozens of roadside stories to inspire your own Route 66 adventure. We are also saddened that two-lane stalwart Bobby Troup has passed on. Bobby and I spent many hours at his home, talking about music and California and the odd turnings in life's journey. His legacy is a special *joie de vivre* and he will be greatly missed.

Happier news is that the Route 66 revival is stronger than ever. Though cherished roadside businesses still close from time to time, the rate has slowed to a trickle. Old and new businesses are thriving all along the route, thanks to over $25 million in annual roadside revenue generated by tourism and attention from international media.

State Route 66 Associations are growing too, as is signage and commitments by state governments to maintain and restore, wherever possible, the old roadway.

So you can ignore those who say that the old road is in danger and must yet be saved. With the enthusiasm of travelers just like you—and fifteen years' work by dedicated Route 66 Associations and roadsiders—that mission has largely been accomplished. Route 66 is alive and well, waiting for you to share in the experience.

Happy touring.

INTRODUCTION
by BOBBY TROUP

Oh, the memories . . . of Route 66 and that special time in America. I recall it all so well.

Before World War II my song, "Daddy," was topping all the charts. In celebration I bought this olive-green Buick convertible for myself and a black Buick sedan for my mother—I was buying everybody Buicks—and it was in that car that my first wife Cynthia and I started for California.

It was 1946 and I was fresh from a combat command in the Pacific with one of the first black Marine Corps units, and I had decided to give myself one year in Hollywood to see if I could really make it as a songwriter.

The first day out we stopped at a Howard Johnson's near Pittsburgh. That was when Cynthia first suggested, quite hesitantly really, that I write a song about US 40. But there didn't seem to be any point to it because we were going to pick up US 66 soon. Cynthia laughed and said, "Get your kicks on Route 66!" The phrase was so great that I began working on the song right away.

By the time we reached Chicago I had half the song written, and I'd measured the distance to L.A. on the map. It was over 2,000 miles. "Route 66" turned out to be one of the best songs I've written, though I didn't realize that at the time.

Many people know that part of the story by now, but what I've never talked about much was the trip itself. US 66 was known, of course, but it was usually called the Middle Route. It was strictly in the business of getting people to California—all the mystique of the road came later.

St. Louis, Missouri was our first big stop. Louis Armstrong was playing a date at the Club Plantation over the first two weeks in February. I knew enough people in the big-band business from writing for Tommy Dorsey, that we managed to get into a standing-room-only crowd. It was a great club, right on the original Route 66.

Not many new cars had come off the post-war assembly lines yet, so we had the road mostly to ourselves. That was just as well because a good part of the highway was absolutely miserable—narrow, just two lanes, and very twisting through the Ozarks and Kansas.

We stopped to see Meramec Caverns, of course. Everybody did. But in Texas our luck with the weather ran out when a blinding snowstorm blew down from the north. The wind was so bad that the snow was blowing horizontally across the road. It would be easy to get hit out there with trucks straying over the line, and there didn't seem to be any letup. The Buick convertible wasn't exactly weatherproof either, so we holed up in Amarillo.

Our car was running all right, but the tires were badly worn and the engine was using a huge amount of oil. I was keeping track and it took seventy-five quarts, in all, before the trip was over.

I was really attached to that old Buick and it was hard for me to sell the thing. But the top was in tatters by then and the engine was beyond salvation. The last time I saw the car was on a weekly auction they once televised in Los Angeles. A pitchman was saying that it had only been driven by a little old lady in Pasadena. But the crowd didn't believe him. There wasn't a single bid and they couldn't even get the Buick's engine to start.

We've all been through a lot since then, but it's wonderful to see the old road being preserved. I am indebted to the highway and all the road fans who love its music. Route 66 has been good to me and I feel honored to be part of a great revival.

That's why I'm so pleased my friend Tom Snyder is adding this collection of roadside tales to his Route 66 guide. Some of these stories are funny or sad. Several are mysterious. But they all say something important about the highway and its people. They speak to the heart of every traveler.

WELCOME TO
THE OLD ROAD

Traveling is about seeing new places, and about pointing a camera at squinting people or at things that usually turn out to be too far away.

Traveling is about spending money on stuff you'd never dream of buying at home. It's about discovering the different and occasionally the bizarre—about finding something adventurous, daring, and even romantic in yourself. It's about expanding your perceptions along with the changing view just beyond the windshield.

Traveling is like racy lingerie, trashy magazines, kitchen gadgets, and auto accessories. None of these are truly necessary, but they all make life a little more interesting, a little spicier than it might otherwise be. Old Route 66 is like that. No longer necessary to efficient cross-country travel, the road has been replaced by nine seamless inter-state highways with no stoplights, no places of special interest, no appealing monstrosities. Just mile-by-mile progress in one direction or another. After the first few hours the ordinariness of it all is like watching a test pattern on television.

But Route 66—ah, Route 66 was never ordinary. From its commissioning in 1926, the first highway to link Chicago with Los Angeles, US 66 was, to townspeople along the route and travelers alike, something special. Soon it was even being called the "most magical road in all the world." And by any standard, that's what it became.

Swinging southwest by west from Lake Michigan, US 66 crossed the rivers, plains, mountains, deserts, and canyons of eight states and several Native American nations before ending 2,448 miles on a corner near the Pacific. Yet like most American highways of the day, the original roadway remained little more than a dusty, transcontinental rut that usually filled with water and mud on the least occasion of rain. In those days, even Lindbergh's solo flight over the Atlantic was easier than a cross-country trek by automobile in the same year. Travelers who made it as far as the Great Mojave paid dearly to load their vehicles onto railroad flatcars rather than risk a breakdown out on the vast desert.

Still, the road that became the Main Street of America was nothing if not commercially inspired. An intense lobbying effort by the original Highway 66 Association soon created, from a patchwork of farm-to-market roads and old trails, a single, all-weather highway. More importantly, the Association transformed that highway into something else as well: *the idea that Route 66 is an extraordinary experience—a destination in itself.*

That idea is what changed a more convenient way to cross the country into a new purpose for going. A few days' travel on Route 66 became a tour of the highway itself and the excitement of being on the road became as important as any arrival. In advertising terms, that's when the sizzle caught up with the steak.

By the mid-1930s, the highway had begun to create its own myth; it grew larger than life. It became *the* way west. First it was John Steinbeck, who recognized a feminine, nurturing quality in Route 66, and termed it "the mother road," forever embedding the highway and the Joad family in the nation's consciousness. After World War II, it was Bobby Troup's turn. His musical Triptik for getting your kicks on Route 66 has since been recorded by nearly everyone from the Andrews Sisters to the Rolling Stones and Michael Martin Murphey. But it was the first great recording by Nat King Cole that changed the way an entire nation would pronounce the name. After Cole's rendition, it would be "root sixty-six" forever. During the 1960s, the road became even more famous, earning top billing in the literate and successful TV series *Route 66*, created by Stirling Silliphant and Herbert B. Leonard and propelled across the continent by Nelson Riddle's magnificent road theme.

In the process, US 66 became much more than a highway. For the millions who traveled her (and the millions more who still want to), the road was transformed from a concrete thoroughfare into a national symbol: a vital life-sign for us all. A pathway to better times—seldom found, but no less hoped for. Route 66 came to represent not only who we were as a people, but who we knew we could be. Not a bad thing to find in a road.

Yet change came to old Route 66, as to all who traveled her. She was abandoned in many places, reduced to the homely duties of "frontage road" in others, her magic double digits were given away, her job taken over by a homogenized, fast-food freeway. With the final stretch of I-40 opened in 1984, and the decision by state transportation officials to remove all trace of Route US 66 markings, the upbeat road rhythms became a dirge. And this time we risked losing a great deal more than just another obsolete highway—this time we risked losing something of ourselves.

But there ought to be a saying that you can't keep a good road down. You may take away her destination, even steal her magic numbers. But you can't keep old Route 66 out of the hearts and thoughts of three generations of road-borne Americans.

Just by driving the old road and visiting with the truly wonderful people to be found along the way, you'll become part of the spirit and the legacy of Route 66 across America. As you follow the updated road maps in this book, you'll find the thin, wavy line that was once Route 66 seems frail, often cut completely through by the double-barreled interstate.

But there's a lot of fire and an embracing warmth in the grand old lady yet. So take everything in, experience the road fully, be a part of what you find. Enjoy every curve, every long, die-cut straight, every place to stop along the way. Re-create for yourself and share with those you love the sweetness of a time gone by. A time to be rediscovered on the Main Street of America. Welcome to the old road.

Welcome to Route 66.

A BRIEF
LOOK BACK

Most of us think of the Auto Club in terms of a magical plastic card that can get us out of the soup when the battery dies on a rainy Monday morning, or when that baldish, left rear tire finally goes flat somewhere west of Barked Knuckle. That's truly unfortunate. Because there is much more to the Auto Club story, and a rich history to boot.

Except for a handful of urban operations and small automotive social clubs, the Automobile Club of Southern California was virtually alone when it was established as a service organization in 1900. Aviation, radio, television, balloon tires, the tin lizzie—tow trucks, certainly—were all in the future. Even the ubiquitous American Automobile Association (AAA) did not make an appearance for another two years.

Indeed, at a time when most road maps were little more than by-guess-and-by-gosh squiggles, the Automobile Club of Southern California was already making highly detailed surveys of major roadways in the United States. Beginning in 1920, the Club undertook charting of both the National Old Trails and Lincoln highways from Los Angeles to New York City and Washington, D.C. Using a roadster equipped with a survey speedometer, compass, inclinometer, and altimeter, a crew of two documented an amazing 25,000 miles of highway in the first year and an equal number in 1921.

The strip maps you see in this guide are based on later refinements of that first—and to this day, astonishing—undertaking by the Automobile Club of Southern California. Today, using the latest in electronic survey methods and digital technology, the Automobile Club of Southern California continues as a major resource in cartographic development.

One last note: Remember that the 1930s ads found throughout this guide are for businesses no longer in operation along the route.

USING THESE
UPDATED MAPS

Each map you find here is a superb example of the cartographer's art. Every representation, with its detailed landforms, rivers, ponds, structures, roadways, and towns, can be invaluable in rediscovering many portions of old (or old, old) Route 66, which have been retired for thirty-five years or more. Even major railroads sometimes move or disappear altogether. But mountains, valleys, and (most) rivers pretty well stay put, and these maps show them clearly. So you're sure to enjoy tracking down the parts of old Route 66 that interest you most, using these maps as your guide. Even in this day of satellite photography and computer enhancement, these beautifully crafted little strips remain a marvel of both information and accuracy.

To assist you in making transitions from the superhighways to old Route 66, *the approximate routes of related interstates appear as parallel lines with I-numbering*. A few nonexistent or ruined portions of old Route 66 have also been deleted where these might be confusing.

Otherwise, each of the strip maps appears here just as it did when originally published. Most are from the 1933 edition of *National Old Trails Road and U.S. Highway 66*. The Santa Rosa–Albuquerque section is drawn from a booklet published after that alignment was completed in 1937. A separate strip map is also used to cover the last segment from Los Angeles to Santa Monica, not included in the 1933 publication.

PLANNING YOUR
ROUTE 66 TOUR

If you're one of the many who have tired of the interstate grind, this guide will introduce you to easy-on easy-off sections of old Route 66. At first, you may have only a couple of hours to spare. That's fine. But if you love the feeling of an old two-lane road, if you want the experience of going back to an earlier time, if you are like the rest of us—travelers who have become enchanted by Route 66—you'll soon be back for the whole tour. In the meantime, it's always fun to do a little mind traveling.

This guide was not designed for coffee-table conversation, however. It will serve you best when kept in the glove compartment or close at hand. It should be well thumbed, brown edged, and stained with juices from your favorite Route 66 cafes and barbecue joints. And if the back cover ends up as a shim for a noisy side window, so much the better. When the pages get really bad, just have the whole thing bronzed. It might be a good way to memorialize all your experiences along the old road.

Now to the most-asked questions about touring Route 66.

Which seasons are best? Unless you are forced by school or work schedules to travel only in summer, you'll enjoy your tour much more during other seasons. October and November are usually wonderful months to travel through the Southwest, with only a small risk of early storms in the Midwest. If you're westbound, that's usually no problem. March and early May are also lovely most anywhere along the route. Winter, too, is a great time to get out of the snow belt and experience the change from midwestern temperatures to the sunny and uncrowded beaches of Southern California. Except for the low deserts where seasonal travel is reversed, discounts of 20 to 25 percent are common for the off-season period from October through April.

Is it safe? If you live with, or have heard about, daily urban violence, this is a natural question. The answer is that Route 66 is as safe today as it was some years ago.

For the most part, it is a highway of small towns and open land and we've heard of no incidents involving travelers. Just observe normal precautions and enjoy your tour.

What about facilities en route? No problem. Even on the long loop away from the interstate in Arizona, the old route is rarely desolate. Food, fuel, accommodations, and other services are usually nearby.

Which direction is best? Plan to drive the highway from east to west if at all possible. Due to the western migration of the American population and the lure of Southern California over the past fifty years, Route 66 is primarily a westbound road. Moreover, because travelers were all spent out by the time they returned east, most tourist businesses and attractions are positioned with that in mind. And since it is too costly to print bi-directional guides, authors and publishers generally present a westbound point of view. So follow other great highways east. But take Route 66 west!

How many days will it take? Because everyone's touring style is different there can be no single answer. But there is a lighthearted way to estimate the time that is amazingly accurate. So grab a pencil and notepad.

As it exists today, Route 66 extends about 2,300 miles from Chicago to the Pacific. Add a hundred miles of honey-I-missed-its and you'll have an even 2,400. That distance can be driven, by college students and assorted crazies, in four days with a radar detector. A more reasonable estimate, what with a little weather and a surprise or two, would be eight days. Let's take that as a base number for a fast trip.

First, select one of the categories below, that fits the primary driver and multiply the eight days by the factor indicated.

Late Starter/Get Loster/Honky Tonker 2.00
Antiquer/Shopper/Sensitive Browser. 1.75
Hobbyist/Museum Freak/Coffee Hound 1.50
Photographer/Poser/Postcard Looker 1.25

Next, for every passenger who belongs to a *different* category, add one day to the number you calculated above; if married to the driver, add another day for argument's sake.

Finally, add two days for each sidetrip to Santa Fe, Grand Canyon, or along the Pacific Coast. If your math is even remotely correct, you should have a total of eight to twenty-four days.

The point is, you'll work it out and have a great time. Don't worry.

What should I pack? A Route 66 tour is simplicity itself, yet travelers always have enough stuff to invade a small country. Unless you *know* you're invited to the maharaja's reception, leave all the sports jackets and dresses home. I carried a navy blazer along on half a dozen crossings and never wore it once. Bring some jeans and light tops and shorts and sneakers in summer, plus a sweater and windbreaker for the rest of the year. Except for socks and underwear, two of anything else is all you'll need. T-shirts? Buy some Route 66 ones when yours get whiffy. Coin-op laundries are also easy to find.

Of course, some people just need to carry a lot of stuff. My family did. We always followed the golden rule of traveling: *Be sure you have enough——take too much.* Now I generally tour the whole country with two cameras and a gym bag. Trust me, it works.

One further suggestion: if you're not an Auto Club member already, you may want to consider joining. Their exhaustive tour book listings of accommodations, plus the excellent state maps they offer, are worth more than the price of an annual membership. And you get road service in the bargain.

Remember only that too much dependence on toll-free reservations and such can deaden the feeling of personal adventure, romance, and discovery that comes with exploring an old road on your own. The aim in this guide is to achieve a balance between touring commentary and your right to find your own way, make your own discoveries, and choose when you need to make time on the interstate. And when you don't.

Even if you're only a closet roadie, you'll be delighted to know that, with few exceptions, old Route 66 can still carry you from Lake Michigan to the California coast.

Most of the towns and much of the original roadway remain, and you'll enjoy seeing the country as you may never have seen it before. You'll also enjoy meeting many of the people who have made this highway their life. They're good folks.

Be sure to say hello for all of us.

MINI-TOURS • RENTALS • DISCOUNTS

Many readers have asked for information on auto rentals, motorcycles, fly-drive-rail options, and discounts available to Route 66 travelers. This new edition covers all these.

Discounts. For many accommodations, services, and attractions from Chicago to Los Angeles, you can do very well on discounts as an AAA member. Through the club's Show Your Card and Save program, you can expect discounts of 10%–20% below prevailing rates. That's more than enough to pay for the membership and result in some hefty savings too.

Cost of a one-year membership ranges from $30 to $72, varying from state to state. Members are entitled to free AAA TourGuides and maps for each state along the route—and we highly recommend them—plus other member benefits.

Other discounts on highway memorabilia are available to members of the US Route 66 Association through Route 66 Collectibles. See page 184.

Auto Rentals. If the prospect of driving over 5,000 miles round-trip is somewhat daunting, consider Route 66 as a fly-drive vacation. Early airline reservations usually qualify travelers for low fares plus discounts on auto rentals. Ask your local travel agent or AAA representative to walk you through the wide array of packages and promotions, however.

That's because rates on auto rental change almost daily—you'll need exact dates simply to get a quote. Yet because so many readers have requested cost estimates, here are some general guidelines.

Prices will always be higher in peak travel seasons and quotes are only good for about 10 days unless you make a reservation. Rental agencies also require a major credit card and a minimum age of 25 for all drivers.

It is generally less expensive to rent through a hotel or downtown office during the week and at an airport on weekends. You may not always find the same selection of vehicles, though, so check on both.

IRS tax forms are simple compared to auto-rental prices and contracts. Be clear about every detail, and know exactly what your personal auto insurance covers before paying additional fees. It can also be cheaper to add special rental-car coverage through your own insurance company.

As this revision goes to press, a 10-day off-season rental of a mid-size automobile with unlimited mileage from Chicago to L.A. ranged from about $300 to over $1,200. One company had a low daily rate, but charged a whopping $1,000 to drop the car off in L.A., so beware. Some companies have no drop-off arrangement at all. But Budget Rent a Car has taken the lead in eliminating the drop-off fee altogether!

Moreover, Budget's fleet includes both sporty cars like the Ford Mustang, and light trucks. This makes a fly-drive-rail vacation a real possibility, with Amtrak's *Southwest Chief* service from Albuquerque passing through exactly the same country as Route 66—often only a few yards from the highway. And, if you consider fuel and lodging costs, Amtrak service can even be less expensive.

A marvelous tour would include a flight to St. Louis or Oklahoma City, with a rental car from there to Albuquerque, Amtrak on to Los Angeles, and return home by air. For shorter vacation times and ease of crossing the desert, especially in the heat of summer and early fall, a fly-drive-rail tour would be just the ticket.

Motorcyle Rentals. Yes! If you're a licensed rider over 25, you can rent a custom Harley-Davidson for your Route 66 adventure. Although motorcycles are not normally available in Chicago (the season is too short), we've located a firm that can provide just the bike you're looking for.

Route 66 Riders is an authorized Harley-Davidson Rental Agency, specializing in custom Harleys at competitive rates. The company is located at 4161A Lincoln

Blvd., in Marina Del Rey, just a few blocks south of the official end of Route 66. They offer everything from Sportsters through Softails and Electraglides, and if you want to celebrate the end of your journey, or life at the beach, bikes can be rented for as little as a half-day.

Again, one-way charges can push the cost up. So a good way to save is by touring with another rider—two machines can be shipped from L.A. and picked up in Milwaukee for the price of one, about $550.

On average, rates are about $150 per day, including tax, basic insurance, leather jackets, and helmets. Packages with unlimited mileage are also available. You must be at least 25 years of age, have a valid motorcycle license, plus a major credit card. Phone them at (888) 434-4473 or (310) 578-0112 for details. They're nice folks to deal with and their machines are first-rate.

California Tours. From a day's run up the beach and through the Santa Monica Mountains to a full-on tour, take time to experience the California coast.

To the north along SR 1, it's 2 to 3 days through Malibu, Santa Barbara, San Simeon, Big Sur, Carmel, Santa Cruz, and Half Moon Bay to San Francisco.

To the south, take the highway around Palos Verdes Peninsula, then continue south through Corona Del Mar, Laguna Beach, and Dana Point. Rejoin 1-5 across Camp Pendleton, then exit at Oceanside for a beachfront run through Carlsbad and on into La Jolla and San Diego, about two days.

Either route is misty and sweet and unforgettable. And both are described in detail in the new *Pacific Coast Highway Traveler's Guide,* second book in this retro-touring series from St. Martin's Press.

PLANNING NOTE: For easy access to sources and up-to-the-minute information covering both Route 66 and Pacific Coast Highway, visit www.sentimentaljourneys.org on the Internet.

Traveler's Guide

1

It's tempting to think of old Route 66, stretching from Chicago to Los Angeles, as a happy accident. After all, her famous double-sixes were little more than that, the road having first been designated Route 60 for a short time. But the truth is that there is a strong Illinois–California connection that predates the road, extending back to the turn of the century. It was then that the route which was to become US 66 was cobbled together from existing pathways. And they really were little more than pathways. Trails, traces, fence-row tracks, farm-to-market roads, and even some private drives were linked with stagecoach routes farther west to create something resembling a continuous roadway. And just in time, too, for the unending stream of tin lizzies being mass-produced by Henry Ford.

Business and personal connections between Chicago and Los Angeles were already established as well. One of Hollywood's very first moviemakers came not from New York but from Chicago. The winter of 1907 had threatened to run Francis Boggs and his tiny film company out of business. Only the interior scenes of Boggs's twelve-minute epic, *The Count of Monte Cristo*, had been shot when the snows ended any hope of outdoor filming. Boggs, his crew, and his players headed west in search of better conditions and a light more suited to the slow film speeds of the day. They found what they needed in Los Angeles—bright sunshine, cheap land, and free scenery. The following year

Boggs moved production to the West Coast for good. Ince, Sennett, DeMille, and others followed, of course, but Chicagoan Boggs had led the way. Even the name *Hollywood* came not from the holly trees that were planted later but from an upstate neighborhood in Illinois.

Of the midwestern states, Illinois has always been the champion trader, track layer, and road builder, with Chicago at its hub—importing and exporting anything movable, anything thinkable. But Chicago need not have lured itself into the trap of comparison. Better to be called Windy City than Second City. For there is nothing whatever second class about Chicago. Its outrageous blend of southern black cool, northern liberalism, and blue-collar ethic, along with its midwestern reserve and commercial might, is sometimes politically awkward—but always in motion.

None can fan the twin flames of devotion and despair quite like the Cubbies. And even Green Bay cannot match the chill factor at Soldier Field during a Bears losing streak. Chicago has exported broad-shouldered poetry, prairie architecture, miles of unfortunate hams, uncounted Studs Terkelisms, a large part of the original cast of *Saturday Night Live*, plus—bet you didn't know this—the Lava Lite, premier icon of the early-plastic 1960s.

These are good things to know, if you're starting out on a tour of old Route 66 from its beginning point. For, in a very real sense, Los Angeles could not have been successfully linked with the eastern seaboard. Even with today's bicoastal management style, Southern California and New York have too little in common. Only Chicago—hunkered down, smack in the middle of America's heartland—could anchor one end of a great, new westering highway that factory workers, farmhands, hitchhikers, businesspeople, teachers, truckers, and songwriters would know as their own. Chicago was, and is, exactly the right place to start.

CHICAGO TO
BLOOMINGTON

First, let's clear up some confusion about the origin of the highway in downtown **Chicago.** Old Route 66 originally began on Jackson Boulevard at Michigan Avenue, a few blocks north of the present-day departure of Interstate (I) 55 from I-90 and 94. After the 1933 World's Fair provided some reclaimed land, the terminus was moved farther east to Lake Shore Drive at the entrance to Grant Park. Then, in 1955, Jackson Boulevard became an eastbound one-way thoroughfare with Adams Street as its westbound counterpart, one block farther north. So the most direct route west is now via the newer Adams alignment.

If you'd like to stay near the beginning of the route for photography and an early start, the Swisshôtel on Wacker Drive offers an exciting view of Michigan Avenue to the south. At more moderate rates, the Best Western Grant Park Hotel on Michigan Avenue at 11th Street is a good choice.

But don't let the adventure begin without giving yourself a send-off celebration and a good meal. The very best place for both is Lou Mitchell's at 565 W. Jackson Boulevard, where they serve breakfast all day, and still give free Milk Duds to each woman customer. This spot has been a well-loved Chicago landmark since 1923 and right on the route for over thirty years. Open from 5:30 A.M. until 3:00 P.M., you can even squeeze in a few minutes early to get a running start on your first day out. Lou Mitchell's is superbly managed, with an atmosphere that is born of both city business and the open road ahead. So bring your maps and guide, find a spot of your own, and be glad that such traditions remain.

It's easy to reach Lou Mitchell's from westbound Adams. Simply turn south on Des Plaines just before the interstate overcrossing, and double back east on Jackson. The restaurant is at Jefferson, with free parking usually available until eight in the morning. And save a Danish for me, okay? We'll be on the road together for 2,400 miles and the bakery here is terrific.

From Adams, just beyond Ashland Avenue, take Ogden

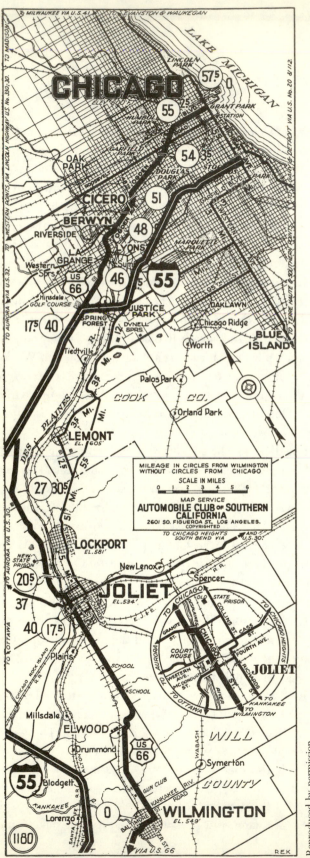

Avenue southwest through **Cicero.** Once a home away from home for Chicago mobsters, Cicero's streets were honeycombed with tunnels allowing gangsters and bootleggers to move unseen from blind pig to brothel, with even Eliot Ness and his Untouchables none the wiser. Cicero now works hard to present a squeaky-clean image. Almost too squeaky. But some of the tunnels are still there. Perhaps there's even one right under the intersection of Ogden and Cicero Avenues. Old Route 66 lies beneath I-55 for the next few miles, and after that you will have a choice. You may jog south on Harlem Avenue, which is State Route (SR) 43 in Lyons, and turn southwest again on Joliet Road to follow the old road into **Joliet.** This is the older route, more historic but also more congested.

Or you may continue straight on SR 126 at Exit 261, pass through the **Village of Plainfield** and turn south on SR 59 to reconnect with I-55 after just 6 miles. This route is newer, with a more open feeling and Plainfield is restoring a vintage look town. Unless construction through Joliet is complete, this may be the better choice.

Continue to the **Wilmington** exit to rejoin the old route. Just north of Elwood, cross the bridge and at one-half mile, jog left then right onto the old two-lane. Watch for a line of weathered telephone poles that often signals an older route and follow Manhattan Road to Mississippi Road, curving back toward SR 53. Rounding the bend, the two-lane becomes Elwood Road and recrosses the newer highway. Continue west on the old alignment into **Elwood** proper. Then follow Douglas until it rejoins SR 53 at the southern end of town.

After entering Wilmington, follow the old route west on Baltimore (SR 53) and continue south through **Braidwood, Godley,** and **Braceville.** Some of the first landmarks of old Route 66 appear along this stretch of two-lane highway, along with several beer-and-skittles roadhouses. South of **Gardner,** as SR 53 swings back north, make a hard left turn to the south and continue on the old two-lane alignment of Route 66. Or continue south to Bloomington on I-55, which closely parallels this route.

Four-lane bypasses for the towns from **Dwight** through **Towanda** were built at the close of World War II, but there are still good sections of older highway to be found east of the interstate, between the newer four-lane and the railroad. The Carefree Motel and a Marathon Oil station are in Dwight, both dating from the 1930s. Near **Cayuga,** look for a photo opportunity to the west where, in a cluster of farm buildings, there is still a barnside ad for Meramec Caverns on Route 66 in Missouri.

From the early days of the old road, Meramec Caverns has been one of the most aggressive and colorful of all highway advertisers. And the cave is a great attraction still, so you may as well start thinking about a stop there. Besides, it's part of traveling to get excited, even to keep asking every few miles if we're *there* yet. You're a card-carrying adult now. You can even stick your feet out of the car window if you want to. Well, for a little while anyway . . . but leave your socks on.

Running a highway business is no easy task. And life can suddenly seem impossible when the highway department announces that the road will be moved. Some folks fold up and quit while others try to hang on. A few call up a special form of creativity born of desperation. Near **Pontiac** stands the Old Log Cabin Inn. Actually, it's a slightly newer version. The old inn fronted on the original Route 66 alignment next to the railroad. But the newer alignment of the highway was going to pass *behind* the place. Even the highway department pitched in and soon the problem was solved. The entire building was jacked up, turned around, and plopped down again—facing the new Route 66.

Continue south, taking care at the short detour just before Normal. You may also encounter some delays as Illinois resurfaces old Route 66 downstate. Be patient, it's needed. **Normal** and **Bloomington** have grown together, so you'll enter on the two-lane, which becomes Pine, turn south on Linden, west on Willow, and south again onto Main Street. When Main becomes one-way northbound, follow US 51 south. Turn west at Oakland, south on Morris, and bear right crossing Six Points Road. Just before the Business Loop, turn right to cross over I-55 then left to follow Beich Road south from town. If you miss and end up on I-55, recovery is easy via Exit 154 to Shirley.

Bloomington has had its share of famous folks. Adlai

Stevenson, a man who demonstrated that a political life can also be one of great public service, lived here. Major Gordon W. Lillie, who became a great Wild West show star as Pawnee Bill, was born here in 1866. And the now-famous surgeon Henry Braymore Blake, M.D., was reared and educated here as well. Colonel Blake was killed on a bright summer day in 1951 when the military air transport on which he was returning from duty in Korea was report-edly downed over the Sea of Japan. Despite pleas by Bloomington visitors, however, the city has yet to dedicate a memorial—or even a small parade—to honor him.

BLOOMINGTON TO ST. LOUIS

Heading south toward McLean on the west side of I-55, be sure to take time for a visit to **Funks Grove,** just beyond **Shirley.** Turn west across the tracks for one of the more photogenic spots you'll find on this part of the route. Look over the old railway depot and the antique antique shop. Then head on across the road, and a little south, for the famous maple syrup plant. If you're planning to travel this way late in the year, however, you'd best get your reservation in early. The Funks have been making this syrup since the 1800s, so they are quickly sold out. And take it from someone who grew up in sugar bush country, this is *excellent* maple syrup. What's more, you'll have a little bit of old Route 66 right there in your refriger-ator when you get back home.

Getting hungry yet? Remember the room you saved (or were supposed to save) for pie? Well, it's almost on your plate. As a long-haul driver would say, just keep the shiny side up and the muddy side down as you head for the Dixie Truckers Home in **McLean.** Built only a couple of years after Route 66 was commissioned in 1926, the Dixie has since been a stop of choice for many traveling this part of the highway. And in all that time, the place has been closed only one day. That was in 1965, when the original Dixie burned down. Today, the Dixie still serves good food and great pie. They also support the movement

in Illinois to revitalize old Route 66. What more could a roadie want?

Leaving the Dixie, remember to keep the happy side up and the chubby side down, following US 136 west for only a short distance. Watch for the old route angling off to the south toward Atlanta. Continue on and enter **Lincoln** via Business Loop 55. Watch for the huge neon palm tree on the west side of Lincoln Parkway at SR 10. It's the Tropics, on the route since 1942, a classic, and still a favorite with both travelers and locals. Follow Kickapoo (recall Al Capp's famous Kickapoo Joy Juice?) to the western jog on Keokuk to Logan, and then onto 5th, Washington, and Stringer. Lincoln is not a big place, so it's fairly easy to get through town. In the Land of Lincoln, this is the only place to adopt his name *before* he became president. Indeed, the town was actually christened by Lincoln. Still a nice place to raise kids.

From this point to well beyond Springfield, this is Lincoln Country. And indeed there are a number of wonderful public attractions honoring the sixteenth president. But there is also a commercial heaviness about much of it. In fact, if you can find some place where Lincoln is not advertised to have worked, stayed, or stood, you might want to phone the Tourist Police with an anonymous tip.

Continuing south, you'll be passing through **Broadwell,** where Ernie's Pig-Hip restaurant once drew a crowd of regular travelers from all along Route 66. The place is closed now, but well before civil rights were acknowledged by law in the US, Ernie took care to make everyone welcome. You didn't have to be of any particular color or persuasion. All you had to be was hungry.

The remnant of a four-lane is still easiest through **Elkhart** and **Williamsville,** though there are sections of the old, old road along here, if you have the time to ferret them out. South of Williamsville, the old road ends and you must enter **Springfield** on I-55. Take the Sherman exit and follow the interstate business loop, which is mostly old Route 66, through town. There are scattered pieces of the old road around the city—one alignment even runs right under Lake Springfield. If the water level is low, the old roadbed is sometimes visible.

Heading south through Springfield on Business Loop

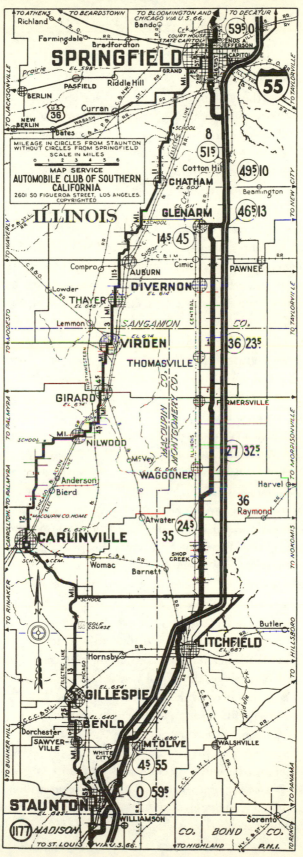

55, you'll have a choice of routes. You can jog west on South Grand and take MacArthur to Wabash to Chatham Road to Spaulding Orchard Road, turning south onto old SR 4. This is an old, old alignment of Route 66, dating from the 1920s, and if you are a true fan of mutant roadbeds, this is the alignment to follow. Although the road is laid out like a series of southerly jumps in a huge game of checkers, the accompanying map is quite consistent with the route through **Virden** and **Carlinville** to **Staunton.**

If you find roadside remnants of Route 66 from the 1930s more interesting, continue on Business Loop 55 and take the Chatham exit. Follow old Route 66 on the west side of the interstate south toward **Glenarm.** Continue straight south to the dead end, then onto southbound I-55, exiting at Divernon. There, turn south again on the westside frontage road to **Litchfield,** home of the Route 66 and Ariston Cafes, both long-term roadside businesses. The Ariston (from the Greek *áristos*, meaning superior) was originally established in Carlinville, along the earliest Route 66 alignment. The family operation moved to the present location in 1935 with the newer routing. The Ariston is more than an excellent place for lunch or dinner, it's an institution.

Continue on through **Mt. Olive,** recrossing to the west side of I-55 opposite Stanton, and straight ahead. Remain on the west side to pick up SR 157. If you're passing through **Hamel** at dusk or during the night, a neon cross on a church there helps speed you safely on your way. It's blue and it's big, but most travelers get an oddly warm feeling from the cross. Even though it is done in neon, there is something tasteful about it—unlike some of the rotating beacons in Los Angeles, which make their churches look more like some place to buy fried chicken. No, this cross is not like that, especially in the rain. It was placed on the front of St. Paul's Lutheran Church by the Brunnworths, whose son, Oscar, had been drowned during the invasion of Italy at Anzio in World War II. Clearly advertising nothing, the cross is simply a comforting tribute.

Follow SR 157 south through **Edwardsville** to the junction with Chain of Rocks Road, just north of I-270. Here, you will have a choice about which route to follow. If you are already familiar with St. Louis or are short on time, you may wish to skirt the city on I-270, rejoining

old Route 66 at the Lindbergh Exit (US 67). Of the old alignments followed by Route 66 across the Mississippi River, only the McKinley Bridge still carries traffic.

Although it's closed to traffic now, Chain of Rocks Bridge is well worth a look. Begun in 1927, it is one of the few bridges in the world with a radical bend in the middle.

From SR 157, take Chain of Rocks Road west beyond **Mitchell.** At the SR 203 junction, cross to the south side of I-270 following Chain of Rocks Road. Continue west over the canal bridge and a brief stretch of dirt road, past the fenced bridge entry, and on down to the river's edge.

Parking can be a problem when the catfish are biting, but the photo opportunity is worth it. Chain of Rocks was repaved for its part in John Carpenter's 1981 film *Escape from New York.* It was, in fact, the bridge over which patch-eyed Kurt Russell made good his escape and upon which Adrienne Barbeau breathed her bosomy last.

If you've decided to take the northern beltline route around St. Louis, return to westbound I-270. To make the McKinley Bridge crossing from **Venice,** take SR 203 south from Mitchell. Continue through **Granite City** and take Nameoki Road (SR 203) to Madison Avenue, which becomes Broadway Avenue in Venice, and then straight across 4th Street and onto the bridge. The McKinley Bridge has been in service for more than eighty years, so you might expect its deck surface to be in very poor shape, and it is. This route through the Venice area also requires caution. It's not a place to have a flat, run out of fuel, or ask questions.

2

MISSOURI

ost place names suffer when they are translated from a mother tongue and later contracted. But not *Aux Arc*, the name of an early Missouri trading post. In the original French, the term is plain, sensible. Like shoes with laces. Yet in its modern form, *Ozark* becomes a mythic word. A mystery. Not dark or ominous but a whisper-word full of timeless secrets. The Ozarks. A place of independent people with soft smiles and stout, natural reserve—backbone of the Show Me State.

Missourians, hands thrust securely into their pockets, can stand for an hour while they wait for you to state your case, make your best offer, or ask directions. In the end, they'll know all they need to about your business and you'll know nothing more about them than you did an hour ago. Some say that comes naturally to folks of solid mining-farming-mountain stock who had to contend with riverboat gamblers, Damn-Yankees, Kansas guerrillas, and the weather hereabouts.

But don't take that to mean that people from Missouri are humorless, for they are not that at all. What other state, with heavy interests in manufacturing, shipping, and the aerospace industry, declares with a straight face that it is also a world leader in the production of corncob pipes? Where else would you find a county government so fed up with the North–South quarrel over slavery that it refused to stand with either faction and instead formed the completely independent Kingdom of Callaway? And along what other stretch of old Route 66 would you be likely to see a hand-lettered sign advertising GUN & DOG SWAP MEET—WOMEN OK (MAYBE)? Not tongue-in-cheek humor exactly, but sly. Very sly.

The larger part of Missouri hangs suspended between its two major cities, St. Louis and Kansas City. Both these cities have dithered over the years, each feeling at various times inferior, each courting greatness, yet often shrinking from the self-surgery that greatness sometimes requires. Through this try-and-try-again atmosphere, old Route 66 plunges diagonally across the state, following the course of the Osage Trail, Kickapoo Trace and, later, the Federal Wire Road, south and west toward Kansas and Oklahoma.

Perhaps more than any other state through which Route 66 passes, Missouri is a region of great contrast. Something of the spirit of *Tom Sawyer* and *The Shepherd of the Hills* is still present here, along with the torment of civil and border wars. Yet there is also a lingering sense of willing endurance handed down from Pony Express riders and the redoubtable Lindbergh.

At a loss for ways to represent the land and culture and people in a single slogan for tourists, the state department of tourism finally surrendered. "Come to Missouri," they finally wrote. "There's no state quite like it." True enough. In spring, when the dogwood is in flower, St. Peter is said to lock Heaven's gates so that Ozark souls do not return to a place of greater beauty.

So if tree-shaded main streets full of memories of old Route 66 are your interest, if you are an antiquer and general poker-about, or if you simply want to cruise smoothly through the roller-coaster hills, be sure to take a little extra time for Missouri. There *is* no other place quite like it.

ST. LOUIS TO WAYNESVILLE

Old Route 66 alignments through **St. Louis** are plentiful but serpentine. So unless you have time to backtrack several times across the city, it's best to take a hybrid route made up of alignments from several periods.

If you have chosen to skirt the city on I-270 to the north, you'll still be following an alignment from the 1930s through the '50s. Old Route 66 lies directly beneath I-270 from Riverview Drive to Lindbergh Boulevard. At Lindbergh (US 67), Route 66 turned south to pass through **Kirkwood** to [New] Watson Road. The traffic is not heavy over this section except during rush hours and Kirkwood is a charming community with much of the feeling of an earlier time preserved. Look for the railroad depot, a classic and still in service.

And if you've an eye for trains and steam locomotives, there are some splendid displays at the National Museum of Transport, just a few minutes away. The museum is a mile or so west of I-270, on Barrett Station Road between Dougherty Ferry Road and Big Bend Road.

Dating from the late 1800s to the final days of steam after Wold War II, the motive power here ranges from early pufferbellies to the giant Santa Fe 2-10-4, which once offered Route 66 travelers the chance to race with a truly fast freight, highballing through the West ("Faster, Daddy, faster . . .") where the old road runs right alongside Santa Fe's rifle-shot tracks. There are lots of other exhibits, too, but the great iron horses still steal the show.

Following your visit, continue northwest on Barrett and turn west on Manchester. Very little of Watson Road and the old Route 66 establishments still exists west of Kirkwood Road. So the far more interesting alignment from the 1920s and '30s is Manchester Road, which can be followed west to **Gray Summit.**

If you plan on taking a through-town route, the McKinley Bridge crossing leads via Salisbury Street to an old business loop. For a side trip, connect with I-70 (posted as east), exiting shortly for the Jefferson National Expansion Memorial Gateway Arch, co-located with several excellent museums, historic buildings, and riverfront attractions. Elegant Eads Bridge, the world's first steel-truss span, is also just to the north. And if you are willing to forgo a couple of hours' sleep, you'll find the bridge especially beautiful in early morning light.

For a convenient route from the park, rejoin the old alignment via Chouteau Avenue just a few blocks to the south and turn west. Continue past Checkerboard Square

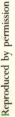

(Were you a Tom Mix radio fan? Can you still sing the Ralston Straight Shooter's theme song?) and turn south again on Tucker (formerly 12th Street), which becomes Gravois Avenue. At Chippewa Street (SR 366), turn west and continue as Chippewa becomes Watson Road.

If you are screaming-for-ice-cream, be sure to stop at Ted Drewes' Frozen Custard. It'll put love in your tummy and most of the flavors will look fine on your clothes, too. The Coral Court, world famous for its Streamline Moderne design—and locally famous as a discreet sin-at-noon palace—is now gone, but a unit has been reconstructed at the National Museum of Transport.

From Kirkwood Road, Watson Road simply disappears under I-44, so turn north on Kirkwood and west again on Manchester Road, which was Route 66 before a newer version of Watson Road was completed in 1932. Or, if you prefer, you can continue on I-44 to the Six Flags exit and follow the business loop to **Gray Summit.**

The interstate route is not without redemption. Missouri has taken the lead by announcing the first major Route 66 park. The 409-acre recreational facility will be on the site of Times Beach—the unfortunate community that was evacuated and leveled as part of a $200 million toxic clean-up. A Route 66 history exhibit and gift shop complement picnic areas, hiking/biking trails and river access. A must-stop. Use Exit 266.

At Exit 261, for **Pacific,** drive a short section of lovely highway to the Red Cedar Inn. When this landmark restaurant opened in 1934, travelers' meals were often served in wayside farmhouses. The Red Cedar Inn has that feeling, with flavorful cookin' and Ozark-friendly service, all under the original family's careful management. Be sure to say hello to Virginia when you stop in.

Continue through Gray Summit and cross over I-44 to the southwest, bear west, recross the interstate, and then follow County AT southwest as it parallels I-44. **Villa Ridge** was once a very big deal along the old highway. And The Diamonds—"world's largest roadside restaurant," according to its owner, Spencer Groff—was once the main attraction here. In the 1920s, he'd run some tiny but highly successful businesses here. One was an all-night banana stand. Undoubtedly, a first in itself. One good thing led to another, however, and Groff put up a building in the shape of a baseball diamond. That's how The Diamonds, a place that served up to a million travelers a year, got its name. The late-1940s restaurant is now the Tri-County Truck Stop, serving a fine road-food buffet to hungry travelers regardless of what they may be driving.

West of Villa Ridge, old Route 66 continues west as North Outer Road to County AH, crossing I-44 to the south side. Continue on South Outer Road and SR 47. At **St. Clair,** recross I-44 to the north side on SR 30 and continue on County WW until it heads north, then continue on North Outer Road to—are you ready yet?— **Stanton,** Missouri. Home of . . . ? That's right, the world-famous Meramec Caverns and alleged hideout of rascally Jesse James and his gang.

One of the best remembered places along the old highway, Meramec Caverns was opened for the tourist business in 1935 by champion roadside entrepreneur Lester Dill. Some locals still say that if Dill had not discovered the caverns, he'd have dug them himself. That's a fair assessment, because Lester B. Dill probably did invent that great American institution—the bumper sticker. So do make time for this attraction. Much of the copy recited by the tour guides hasn't changed since the 1930s. And if you don't happen to know who Kate Smith was, this is as good a place as any to find out.

Crossing to the south side at Stanton at the junction of County JJ and County W, continue west on South Outer Road. In **Sullivan,** keep an eye out for the grand old Shamrock Motel structure. Then continue on the south side through **Bourbon,** where the main street is Old Highway 66. Actually, the name Bourbon is something of a misnomer since this is wine country.

If you missed Meramec Caverns or are a closet spelunker, Onondaga Cave, another old Route 66 attraction, is just south of **Leasburg.** In **Cuba,** be sure to take notice of or stay at the Wagon Wheel Motel. It's well kept and vintage Americana. All it lacks is one of those mirrored globes on a pedestal out front to go with the elves. By now, it may even have one of those.

From Cuba, continue on County ZZ and KK into **St. James.** This area, **Rosati** especially, is known for its table

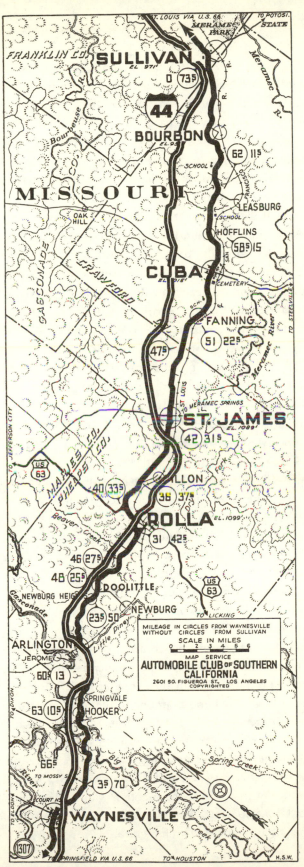

TO ST. LOUIS VIA U.S. 66.
TO POTOSI.
STATE

MERAMEC
PARK

FRANKLIN CO.

SULLIVAN
EL. 971'
0 73⁵

Meramec R.

Bourbeuse Cr.

44

BOURBON
EL. 931'

62 11⁵

Osage Cr.

SCHOOL

LEASBURG

MISSOURI

OAK
HILL

SCHOOL

HOFFLINS
58⁵ 15

CRAWFORD CO.

CUBA
EL. 915'

GASCONADE CO.

CEMETERY

TO STEELVILLE.

SCH

FANNING
51 22⁵

Meramec River

47⁵

TO MERAMEC SPRINGS
ST. LOUIS

ST. JAMES
EL. 1089'

42 31⁵

TO JEFFERSON CITY

MARIES CO.

PHELPS CO.

US 63

40 33⁵

DILLON
36 37⁵

Dry Fork

Beaver Creek

ROLLA
EL. 1099'

31 42⁵

46 27⁵

48 25⁵

DOOLITTLE

US 63

NEWBURG HEIGS

Gasconade

DOOLITTLE

NEWBURG

23⁵ 50

TO LICKING

MILEAGE IN CIRCLES FROM WAYNESVILLE
WITHOUT CIRCLES FROM SULLIVAN

SCALE IN MILES
0 1 2 3 4 5 6

Little Piney

ARLINGTON

JEROME

60⁵ 13

TO DIXON

MAP SERVICE
**AUTOMOBILE CLUB OF SOUTHERN
CALIFORNIA**
2601 SO. FIGUEROA ST., LOS ANGELES
COPYRIGHTED

SPRINGVALE

63 10⁵ HOOKER

Big Piney

66⁵

Roubidoux River

TO MOSSY S

TO ELDON

3⁵ 70

Spring Creek

PULASKI CO.

WAYNESVILLE

1307

COURT HS

TO SPRINGFIELD VIA U.S. 66.
TO HOUSTON

H.S.W.

grapes. If that strikes an appetite chord, plan to stop at one of the little grape stands along old Route 66. Only a few of the older stands remain, and there was a move afoot by the Missouri Department of Transportation to close even the last of these tiny stands down. It seems that people still like to stop, and now that the interstate makes it so difficult to get to the old road, folks just pull to the side of I-44 and visit the stands on foot. Yes sir, sure does sound like it's the grape stands' fault, doesn't it?

Just beyond St. James, there is a break in the old route, so rejoin I-44 or cross to the north side via SR 8 and 68 and continue. At **Rolla,** Route 66 Motors is a great place to stop for a soda. There's plenty of highway memorabilia and always some classic Detroit Iron out front. Through town, the easier route to follow is Business Loop 44, which was a late alignment of old Route 66. Leaving town, follow Martin Spring Drive, which doubles as the south-side service road, and continue on to **Doolittle** (established near **Centerville**).

The town was named for former air-race winner Jimmy Doolittle, who once bolstered sagging morale in the United States by coaxing a tiny flight of sixteen standard-issue army B-25 bombers off the pitching deck of the USS *Hornet* for a raid on Tokyo, just a few months after the attack on Pearl Harbor. It wasn't a mighty blow, but it was a good sharp thumb in the eye at a time when not much was going right for us. As you drive down Doolittle's main street today, say a little word of thanks that guys like Jimmy are around when they're needed.

Approaching **Arlington,** it's necessary to take I-44 for a short distance. For a real old-road treat, however, exit at County J southbound and continue west on County Z. Then turn south at the first opportunity before Big Piney River. You're now right in the crook of **Devils Elbow,** a section of highway famous among Route 66 roadies for its river-bluff scenery and a lovely old steel-truss bridge built in 1923. There's no traffic on this loop, so take time for a stroll and perhaps a picnic lunch. Continue west to return to the County Z four-lane and roll on toward **St. Robert.**

Cross to the north at the junction with Business Loop 44 and continue into **Waynesville,** where there's some interesting Romanesque architecture.

WAYNESVILLE
TO JOPLIN

From Waynesville, follow SR 17 south across the interstate and through **Laquey.** Where SR 17 heads south, follow County AB west into **Hazelgreen.** Continue on the south-side frontage road toward **Sleeper,** cross to the north side at County F, and follow the north frontage road into **Lebanon.** The famous Munger Moss Motel is here, a Route 66 tradition with great neon and hospitality to match.

Joining County W, you will find a fairly long run that gets well away from the interstate almost all the way into **Springfield**—and it's a beautiful drive through unspoiled farmland and small communities. At **Phillipsburg,** cross I-44 to the south and follow County CC and OO through **Marshfield** and past Buena Vista's Exotic Animal Paradise, a ranch-sized spread of wild animals and rare birds. From **Strafford,** continue on OO (SR 744), which becomes Kearney Street in Springfield.

Springfield—"Queen City of the Ozarks"—is worth a browse, especially if you're doing a little photography or are interested in period architecture. From Kearney, turn south on Glenstone Avenue, then west onto St. Louis and College Streets. After a few blocks, you'll notice the Shrine Mosque, a local wonder and an old Route 66 landmark. If you can imagine the Grand Ole Opry in Nashville (or your old grammar school) as it might have been designed by an itinerant Arab architect, you'll have a pretty good image of the mosque. It's wonderful, and in its day hosted some of the biggest acts around.

Farther west, you'll also pass the old calaboose on Central Square, near where Wild Bill Hickok killed Dave Tutt in one of those provoked shoot-outs for which the American West is so famous. As this story goes, Hickok had lost heavily to Tutt in a poker game. To buy time (literally), Hickok had given his pocket watch to Tutt to hold, with the express understanding that the watch would not be seen in public. Too embarrassing to Hickok, you see. But Tutt wore it anyway, Hickok killed him outright—there are plaques in the square to mark where each stood—and everyone settled down to watch Hickok's

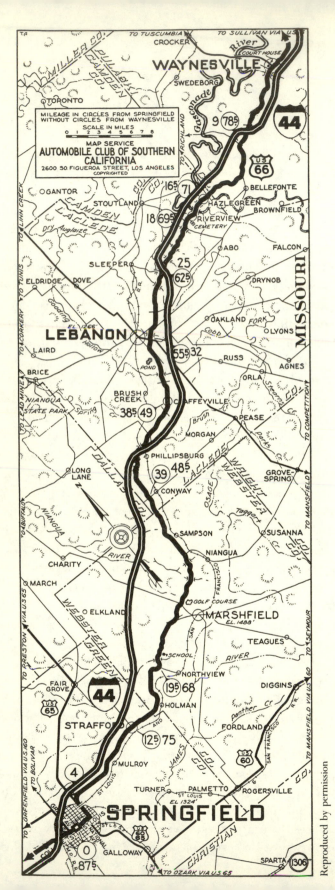

MILEAGE IN CIRCLES FROM SPRINGFIELD
WITHOUT CIRCLES FROM WAYNESVILLE
SCALE IN MILES
0 1 2 3 4 5 6 7 8
MAP SERVICE
AUTOMOBILE CLUB OF SOUTHERN
CALIFORNIA
2600 SO. FIGUEROA STREET, LOS ANGELES
COPYRIGHTED

trial. The verdict was self-defense. But no one seemed to notice that, with Tutt now dead, Hickok had his watch back and no longer owed anything on his gambling debt.

Heading on out of town on the Chestnut Expressway, you may ponder such matters. You also might give some thought to the old stories about how Ozark folk have often been accused of poor bloodlines due to excessive intermarriage. And that might even have been partially true at one time. But consider this: Springfield represents the gene pool that produced none other than Kathleen Turner. With her now-unchallenged acting ability, her smoldering try-it-if-you-dare sexuality, and her down-home beauty, the rest of the country would do well to look into the records here. As genetic codes go, Springfield has a line that is unbeatable.

The section of old Route 66 from Springfield west is a real treat. From **Halltown**—an interesting stop for antiquers—continue west through **Paris Springs Junction** for a cruise on old, old Route 66, rather than jogging south onto SR 96. At the junction with County N, cross to the south of SR 96. Turn west from County N at the first intersection and cross the old steel-truss bridge. Continue through Casey's Corner at what was once Spencer, cross to the north of SR 96 at the stop, and continue toward Carthage.

The town names along this stretch of Route 66 sing a special song in passing: **Albatross, Phelps, Rescue** ... **Log City** and **Stone City** are only shadows of what they were. Indeed, from this section of the old route on west, through parts of Oklahoma, Texas, New Mexico, and Arizona, the number of abandoned businesses and highway attractions increases greatly. In some ways, that's a sad fact. But there is a more cheerful view, championed by observers like John Brinkerhoff Jackson, that there is a great need for relics like these.

Since we can only experience history through our imaginations, they suggest, the ruins we encounter serve as vital props for any journey of the mind in time. In viewing some roadside ruin, then, we are better able to re-create for ourselves the period in which it stood. An interesting thought—that by seeing clearly what remains, each of us gives some ruin a second life. A chance to exist again, as it once was, in the projection of our mind's eye.

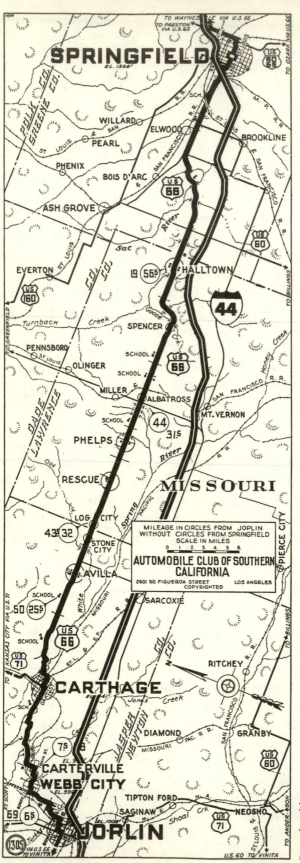

Just knowing this can make the traveling more passionate, the seeing more profound, as you make your way along this old road—which is itself a relic. Yet a relic that you may revive, if only for a moment, by your passing.

Eight-tenths of a mile after **Avila,** beyond the Victory Baptist Church, jog left, then right again along a line of old telephone poles. At the Y stop sign, jog right, then left.

Carthage is next and it, too, is special. A businesslike county seat, it is peopled with individualists of the first rank—the notorious Belle Starr was born here. There is also a strong, creative thread in Carthage that seems to go way back. Still following SR 96, take at least a moment for the town square and the classic Jasper County Courthouse. The clock has been reinstalled after taking the cure for striking thirteen too often. And the courthouse lawn looks pretty good, too. Remember the Missouri sense of humor? Carthage does. Some years back, when the lawn was redone, someone slipped turnip seed into the replanting mixture. The grass was only mediocre, but it was a bumper turnip crop for embarrassed officials.

Entering Carthage on Central Avenue, you'll have a choice. If you're a Bed & Breakfast fan, turn north on Garrison, west on Centennial, and go three blocks to Grand. On your right, at 1615, is the Grand Avenue Inn, a lovingly restored Queen Anne Victorian home, now listed on the National Register. It's charming and even comes with an occasional ghost. Once a cigar-smoking anti-feminist, the friendly apparition has apparently seen the error of his ways and now contends himself with fixing popcorn in the microwave at odd hours. Definitely worth an overnight.

To continue through Carthage from Central, turn left on Garrison and right on Oak Street. Cross US 71, then turn left at the stop. Continue to the T, turning left on Pine, then right onto Main Street in **Carterville.** Follow Main through the S-curve and enter **Webb City,** following Broadway to Madison Street. Then turn left and continue on US 71 to **Joplin.**

Peaceful Joplin sits atop countless abandoned mining tunnels and a rough history—beginning with a two-town rivalry. A local judge and his friend, a Methodist minister named Joplin, had settled a nice, lead-rich town, when a

competing town called Murphysburg sprang up just across
Turkey Creek.

The judge got himself all riled up about that, and the
other town's developer, Murphy, got counterriled. Soon
someone brought in a bushwhacker called Three-Fingered
Pete. Then, someone else hired a brawler called Reckless
Bill, and everybody began having at it on a regular basis.
Mining got all mixed up with religion, which got all mixed
up with the law and the egos of both towns. In the end,
it became such an awful mess that the state legislature
stepped in, Siamesed the two towns under the single name
City of Joplin, and told everyone to behave themselves or
they wouldn't get a railroad.

So things settled down quickly and the miners returned
to their labors all along this old section of the route. In
fact, they worked so hard and long that the road itself
developed a habit of falling into abandoned tunnels. Several
detours have been necessary since a cave-in of the road
in 1939. And as this is being written, there are no new
detours near Galena or down the highway. Still, drive
softly—and when you walk, don't stamp your feet. You
might fall right on through to Tienamen Square.

The easier route through Joplin follows US 71 to SR
66 west. Near the border you notice places like Dixie
Lee's Dine and Dance. Along with Dutch's Top Hat and
Dana's Bo Peep, the last-chance saloon recalls the time
when Kansas was dry. It's no place to go now, though,
so save your two-step for Texas.

West of Joplin, watch for a sign: OLD ROUTE 66 NEXT
RIGHT. The newer SR 66 alignment continues on to Kansas,
but a turn here will put you on another rare, surviving
section of the original route. There's a nice resurrected
feeling about these few miles, which have somehow found
protection through local use.

3

KANSAS

There are only a dozen miles of old Route 66 in Kansas. But they are part of a saw-toothed run from Joplin, Missouri, to Vinita, Oklahoma, that's truly a crackerjack stretch of highway and history. If you've ever wondered why all the old-timers seem to have huge, nautical compasses mounted in their cars or camper cabs, one look at the map for this part of old Route 66 will provide the answer. When you're on a road that zigzags along section lines rather than following a more direct course, it's easy to guess your direction only when it's early or late in the day. The rest of the time you'd better have some other means of knowing which way you're headed.

All of which fits with the old Middle American tradition of never admitting that you don't know something. Most people who grew up from Ohio to Oklahoma know not to ask directions of strangers or service station attendants. Instead of saying that they don't know (when they don't), well-intentioned midwesterners will just give you the most plausible answer they can think of. And it rarely has anything to do with accuracy.

There are a couple of other things to remember as you roll from southern Missouri on into Kansas and Oklahoma. The first is that this area is pretty close to the buckle on the Bible Belt, so you'd best save any snappy ecumenical jokes you have for later. The other thing is to think twice before ordering Italian in these parts. Oklahomans, for example, take their religion and the way their meat is cooked pretty seriously. There are more churches and barbecue joints between the Kansas border and Oklahoma City than some people see in a lifetime. On other matters, excepting football perhaps, Oklahomans are far more laid back.

It's a little different just the other side of the line. In Kansas, they tend to take *everything* seriously. It's not a place to cut up much. Especially in a restaurant at Sunday brunch.

Some of this traces right back to the kind of righteous single-mindedness with which issues have been settled here. People who got caught in the sweeping crossfire between Quantrill's Raiders and the Jayhawkers, during the Civil War period, quickly learned that most everything about life could get serious in a hurry. Later, as the labor movement was beginning in the zinc and lead mines of this region, both the company goons and militant union members took the matter right into the streets. There were times during the mid-1930s when old Route 66 itself ran red, usually with the blood of determined strikers. This is country that has been cleared, farmed, and mined the hard way. And parents have taught their children well.

But a hundred years of conflict in this little corner of Kansas has produced something of great value to the traveler. The people here, along the old road, are as clear and honest and forthcoming as can be found anywhere. What's more, they have a sense of history and a knowledge of themselves which sets them apart.

No one dawdles much here. Work still comes before much else. Of all the states through which old Route 66 passed, Kansas was among the first to see that the highway was properly paved in concrete. The towns here—Galena, Riverton, Baxter Springs—are also among the quietest and most serene you'll find. Take a stroll down by one of the rivers. Walk along a neighborhood street. Listen to the crickets and the screen doors. There are only a few miles of Kansas on the old route, but this place is a big part of the true America we all carry somewhere in our hearts.

It's no wonder Dorothy was so happy to be home again.

GALENA TO
BAXTER SPRINGS

Continuing on the older alignment through **Galena,** turn south on Main Street. Long before Prohibition, when the mining boom could still be heard, this was called Red Hot Street in Galena. And it was that, no doubt about it. The saloons and bawdy houses stayed open twenty-four hours a day, keeping the miners picked clean from payday to payday.

In the beginning, the town of Empire had richer mines than Galena. So, to prevent unwelcome Galenans from making a daily beeline for the better diggings, the protective folks of Empire built a high fence of timbers along the town's border. Galena waited some months until the entire fence was completed, then simply burned it to the ground—so much for the stockade concept. Later, when the mines in Empire began to play out, Galena annexed the town. Departing Galena-Empire, continue on SR 66.

In **Riverton,** about four blocks after crossing the Spring River, watch for Eisler Brothers' General Store to your right, located on the route since 1925. Nice, helpful folks. After that get ready for your zig-zag driving adventure as the old road makes a dozen ninety-degree turns across Kansas and eastern Oklahoma.

West of Riverton, watch for the last remaining rainbow-style, concrete-truss bridges—this one generously supplied with youthful commentary. Formally named Brush Creek Marsh Arch Bridge, travelers have been calling it Graffiti Bridge for years. Names don't exactly go up in lights around here, but this span seems to be a marquee for locally sown wild oats. The bridge was threatened recently, but the state Route 66 association made a great save and you can still drive over it.

To check the roster as well as follow the old road, keep heading west after the four-lane ends, along a line of aging telephone poles. At US 69A, turn right into Baxter Springs.

In **Baxter Springs,** you'll find Murphey's Restaurant and the charming Cafe on the Route, housed in the former Baxter Bank along with The Little Brick Inn. Both restau-

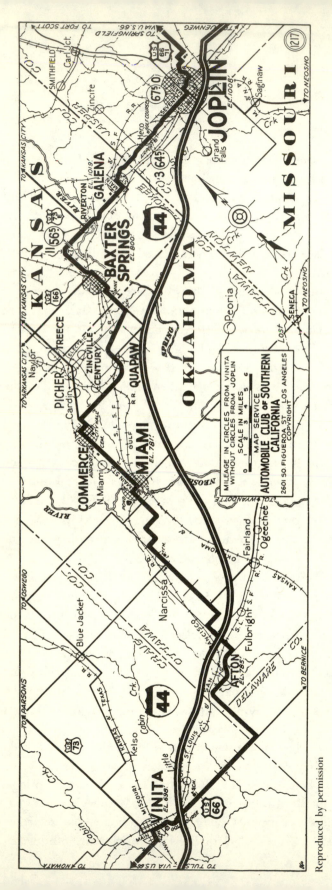

Reproduced by permission

rants have been recommended and the inn offers complimentary breakfasts for guests. But don't let the locals jaw
you too much about the great Jesse James bank heist of
1876. Historians say it didn't happen. The notorious robber was up to no good, all right, but he was somewhere
else.

4

OKLAHOMA

When you talk about outlaws in Oklahoma, it's important to distinguish between regular outlaws and elected outlaws. The state has certainly had more than its share of both. First came all the sod-busters who jumped the line early during the great Land Rush. They undoubtedly set the trend for everybody. Later, when some political hustlers decided that Oklahoma City would make a more profitable center for state government, they simply stole the Great Seal from the existing capitol in Guthrie and hauled it on down to its present site.

One result is that good outlawing became something of a fifth estate in Oklahoma.

Like many of the better class of outlaws, Jesse James and his pals started out in Missouri, but spent a lot of time in these parts. So did Pretty Boy Floyd, an Oklahoman from age five, who soon became a Robin Hood of the 1930s. An expert in the bank-robbing business, Pretty Boy always found time to tear up whatever farm mortgages he could find around a bank. And when on the lam, it is said that he would pay poor farm families for a meal—and silence, of course—with a $1,000 bill.

All across the state, Depression-ridden people understood his motives and were cheered by his exploits. So they defended Pretty Boy and cared for him as their own. When the hapless Floyd was finally gunned down by the FBI, twenty thousand mourners turned out for his burial.

It was the biggest funeral Oklahoma has ever seen. As for Ma Barker and her sons, together with Bonnie Parker, Clyde Barrow, Machine Gun Kelly, and the rest of the outlaws-turned-killers, good riddance. No folk songs are sung about them. None need be.

For many Route 66 travelers, Oklahoma has often been no more than a place to be driven through quickly in order to get to the good stuff farther west. Too bad for them. Because Oklahoma, once truly seen and fully experienced, is one of the most beautiful—and most open-handed—places to be found anywhere. Cyclists and hikers could do no better than pedal or hoof their way through the gently rolling country from the Kansas border to Oklahoma City.

In the western reaches of the state the land is even more beautiful, lying rumpled in all directions like a giant designer bedsheet, small farms and friendly towns among the creases. More attractive to automobile drivers or motorcyclists than to ten-speed riders, perhaps, but magnificent nonetheless.

For real pit-barbecue freaks, however, the entire state is a groaning board. Closet cases of smoke fever may be forced out into the open, and all but the most devout vegetarians will be sorely tested. So you may as well learn the tune: Get your ribs on Route 66.

The remarkable thing is that in Oklahoma as nowhere else, art and architecture go hand in hand with folk history, down-home hospitality, and the sweetness of the green-on-red land. Truly the birthplace of old Route 66, Oklahoma is well worth knowing. Take some time here. Let the people of Oklahoma get to know you, too.

QUAPAW TO
OKLAHOMA CITY

Nearly all of old Route 66 has been preserved and remains in daily use throughout eastern Oklahoma. Since the interstate turnpike is a toll road here, most local and regional travel is done on the Free Road—old Route 66. And an excellent highway it is, too. You'll have little difficulty following this unbroken 260-mile section of the old road as it meanders along from the Kansas border to Oklahoma City.

From Baxter Springs, follow US 69 south into **Quapaw.** If it's coming on nighttime, you may be able to do a little ghost-busting here. For one and a half miles east of Quapaw, on a bluff called Devil's Promenade near the Spring River, is the home of Spooklight, an appartition that sometimes drew as many as a thousand cars per night during the peak spook season. Spooklight (no joke here) appears as a dancing, bobbing, rolling ball of light, seen in these parts regularly for years. Sometimes Spooklight has even been seen entering parked cars.

There are lots of theories, but thus far nothing approaching an adequate explanation. Scientists and army technicians of nearly every stripe have tested this and that, but to no avail. One of the better technical theories is that Spooklight is really only a wandering, atmospheric refraction of headlights on the nearby highway. But that falls a little short when it is recalled that Spooklight was first seen by the Quapaw Indians in the mid-1800s. Not exactly a lot of cars around back then. Undaunted by a lack of theoretical structure, Spookie just keeps on hanging out here. To nearly everyone's delight.

Unless you're spooked, follow US 69 south then west from Quapaw and jog through **Commerce,** home of Mickey (the Commerce Comet) Mantle. Entering town southbound, jog west on Commerce and south again on Main Street, heading on down to **Miami** (pronounced *My-am-uh*).

Continue through Miami on Main Street, and if possible, take time for a look at the Coleman Theater.

From Miami, follow US 69 through **Narcissa,** join. US 60, then cross under the turnpike, and continue to **Afton.** Because so much tourist business has been lost to through traffic on the interstate, only a few attractions have remained open. The Buffalo Ranch is one of them. A petting zoo, barbecue, and buffalo, too. What more could the imagination desire? A llama or a yak? They've got 'em and it's worth a stop.

In Afton, an interesting spot for collectors of nearly any

ilk is the saddle shop, across the street and just east of the old Palmer Hotel. Here you'll find a whole wall of matchbooks, some dating back fifty years or so. None are for sale, but that can't stop you from making a bid on the wall itself.

From Afton, continue south, then west on US 60. **Vinita** is next, named for Vinnie Ream, the sculptress whose rendering of Abraham Lincoln now stands in the nation's capital. Through Vinita, follow US 60 to the junction with SR 66 just before **White Oak.** Then continue southwest on the Free Road into **Chelsea,** the very first oil-patch town and one of the few to have a perfectly preserved example of a Sears mail-order house. It is a private residence, however, so take care not to disturb if you stop by for a look.

Farther south, the village of **Bushyhead** is gone now. But **Foyil** is snug enough, with a nice loop of old, old Route 66, in its original pink concrete, curving through town. Even more interesting is Galloway's Totem Pole Park, a few miles east on SR 28A, where you can see the results of that rare flash of artistic genius some roadside entrepreneurs find in themselves. Take along plenty of film, though. The place is a challenge to portray.

On down the road, **Claremore** is worth some extra time for a visit to the Will Rogers Memorial. Claremore is also the hometown of Lynn Riggs, author of *Green Grow the Lilacs*, on which the Pulitzer Prize–winning *Oklahoma!* is based. Entering town, angle west at the first signal and continue parallel to SR 66 on J. M. Davis Boulevard. This is the old route and motel row in Claremore. The Claremore Motor Inn, though not a real landmark, is comfortable and a good place to collect road stories from the former highway patrolman at the desk. Also, keep a nose-scan going for The Pits. It's on the left and one of the better barbecue places around. Also, if time permits, check out the Davis Gun Museum. Even people who don't like guns are often impressed, and it is a whale of a collection.

Continue southwest, rejoining the Free Road. After the highway bends west, watch for the nonidentical twin spans over the Verdigris River. Most everyone feels compelled to photograph this odd couple of bridges—some locals

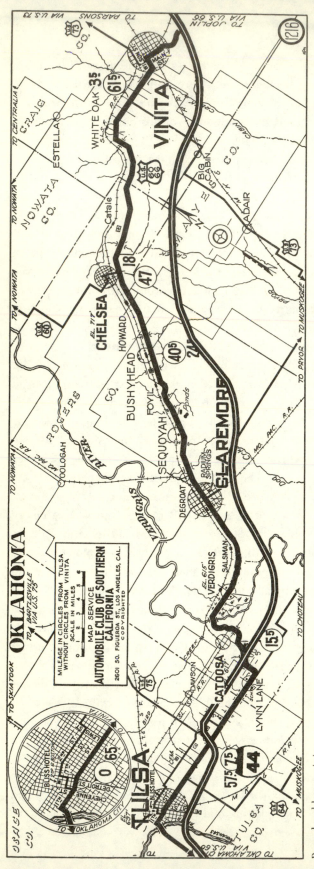

even call them Felix and Oscar—and more than a few travelers are bothered by the difference. But, then, who would notice these structures at all if they matched?

Just a few miles farther, you'll cross Spunky Creek. There was even a Fort Spunky here at one time, and though the name sounds a bit like *Lassie Joins F Troop*, this was once very wild territory. It took spunk to live around here very long.

Cresting the next hill, watch for the old Blue Whale Amusement Park on the right. It may only be a photo opportunity now, but who knows? **Catoosa** has grit as well as a name referring to People of the Light. It's not clear, though, if the Cherokees were seeing the same kind of light as the Quapaws. Across the highway, check out Arrowwood Trading Post. It's uncrowded with a good selection of Indian art from most tribes.

Nearing **Tulsa,** the Free Road can be crowded, so keep a sharp eye out for the SR 167 junction. Tulsa is interesting, so you may want to take the city route. Otherwise, enter I-44 and continue until Sapulpa. If you'll be touring Tulsa, take 193rd Avenue (SR 167) south and turn west again on 11th Street. Admiral Place is an alternative alignment but less interesting overall. Watch for the Metro Diner, just past the stadium at Tulsa University. A little farther on, there's the Route 66 Diner, a bit west of the big Bama Pies building on the north side. Both are fairly new restaurants and are already becoming landmarks for Route 66 travelers. Continuing west on 11th Street, notice the old Warehouse Market, a marvelous piece of art deco and a possible center for neighborhood restoration and redevelopment.

Just beyond Peoria Avenue, 11th bends southwest and becomes 10th Street. Follow the S-curve into 12th Street. Then, at the stop, turn south and follow Southwest Boulevard across the bridge. You may take Southwest Boulevard into **Sapulpa,** if you wish. A quicker and easier route is to rejoin the Free Road just before Southwest becomes Sapulpa Road and bends west. The overpass to 60th Street will take you across to the east side of I-44. Follow signs for the Free Road (SR 66 and 33) toward Sapulpa where the older alignment returns. There's no advantage to the turnpike here since SR 66 is very well maintained.

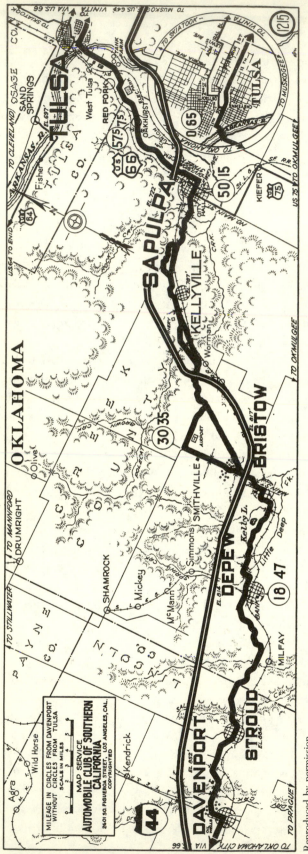

Like Tulsa, Sapulpa has learned to use art cosmetically. Empty store windows become display points for photographic prints. Boarded-up windows in the side of a two-story building become a hand-painted triptych. If you're getting hungry, Norma's Cafe—run by the real Norma—has been serving roadies for years on the corner of the intersection leading west into town on Highway 66.

Departing Sapulpa, watch for an old steel-truss bridge off to the right, about a mile west of town. It's just beyond an intersection marked, curiously enough, Highway 66 and Old Highway 66—perhaps the only acknowledgment of both alignments anywhere in the country. The bridge is especially photogenic with its well-preserved, red-brick deck. Continue on the older alignment beyond the bridge, if you like. It's easy to rejoin SR 66 a few miles farther on, at SR 33.

From Sapulpa through **Kellyville, Bristow,** and **Depew,** there are a number of abandoned sections of old, old Route 66 on the northwest side of the Free Road, some of which can be driven for short distances.

There are also a couple of very nice loops of older alignment, beginning about two miles beyond Kellyville. The first is just past the interstate overpass and rates a slow, top-down drive. There's also another angular section a few miles farther on. It's said that there was once an old airfield along the west leg of this loop. No one has spotted it yet, though. Maybe, you'll be the first. So do some exploring and find your own favorite little tree-shaded country lane. Remember to keep an eye out for lines of weathered telephone poles and old cuts through the trees.

Rolling on into **Stroud,** be sure to check out the Rock Cafe. For years it has been a twenty-four-hour must-stop for travelers through this area. Down the street, 66 Antiques is worth a browse. If the name Stroud sounds a little tough for this sleepy little town now, it's because the place once really was tough. Cattle drovers shipped from here, the nearby Indian Territory was dry, and a string of bars made lots of money selling hooch of questionable character to everybody. Now Stroud is the kind of place where, if you are doing a late wash, you lock up the laundromat after yourself. Nice town.

Approaching **Davenport,** continue straight at the curve for the center of town. Locals take some pride in their rolling streets here. Main is known as Snuff Street—"drive a block and take a dip." Beyond Davenport, the old route heads on into **Chandler.**

Entering Chandler on First Street, the Lincoln Motel on the right has been meticulously maintained since it was built in 1939. And angling south on Manvel, you can gas up at a vintage station. Midway through town, there's the Lincoln County Museum on the right, with its striking redstone exterior and a Route 66 collection. There's also a fine old bakery and Granny's restaurant, both good. But if you're on BBQ time, you can't do any better than P.J. Bobo's. Leaving town southbound, her place is at the bottom of the hill at the hard turn. It's yumful. So be sure to take along some homemade sauce. And if you're done with that slaw, pass it on over, would you? Umh-umh. Best way to hit the road west.

If you're driving something like a Mustang GT or a Corvette, there are some perfectly banked left and right sweepers through this section that can make you cry for more good old roads. Clearly, this highway was designed by men who drove, not by men who budgeted. And it's not hard to tell the difference in the result, is it?

At **Arcadia,** make a slow circle through this little town. It still has that early 1930s feeling. The famous round Barn has been completely restored, due in no small part to Route 66 travelers who have chipped in their dimes and dollars to help out the dedicated preservationists here. The exterior is fine now, and the interior dome is absolutely mind-boggling.

From Arcadia, continue west, but take care. This section of road has not been well maintained in the past. Cross I-35 and head on into **Edmond,** now a northern suburb of Oklahoma City. Little of the old Route 66 feeling remains here. But Edmond is a college town, enjoys a lovely campus, and is a pleasant place in which to shop or take care of business before the run down to Oklahoma City. If you plan to bypass Oklahoma City, however, it's easier to take I-35 in, junction with I-44, and continue west to the Yukon exit.

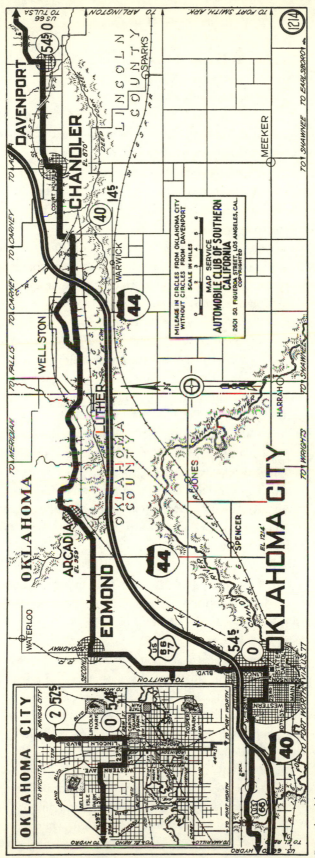

OKLAHOMA CITY
TO TEXOLA

An overnight in Edmond will be quieter and less expensive than the city. The Stratford House, on the route at 1809 E. Second Street, has always been pleasant and there's a laundromat across the street if you're feeling grubby. Continue westbound on Second Street in Edmond, then turn south on Broadway (US 77).

Oklahoma City, like Chicago and Los Angeles, was not much influenced by the highway, so there is comparatively little to experience in the way of Route 66–era businesses or attractions here.

If you do choose the full city loop, follow Broadway south, jogging east at the Kelley Avenue exit and south again. Jog west on 50th Street to Lincoln Boulevard (US 71) southbound, skirt the capitol, and take 23rd Street west. Then turn north on Classen to I-44 for a simple connection to Route 66 west.

But there's a micro-tour that will give you a sense of the city, plus a great photo opportunity, and a neat shop to visit. Just head west on I-44 from the US 77 junction, exiting at Classen Boulevard. Continue south to 25th Street and the giant Townley Dairy milk bottle—truly a classic in commercial architecture. Morning or late afternoon gives the best lighting, so you may want to pick up a few things at Kamp's Grocery, a long-term Route 66 survivor at 1310 NW 25th. Or if you're ready for a bite, the Classen Grill at 5124 Classen is an excellent choice. Good service, too, but closed Mondays. And if you're doing veggies, the Gardenburger is terrific.

Now hang a U-turn and head back up to the top of Classen for a spiffy (and climate-controlled) shop. Transition to westbound Northwest Highway (SR 3A) and go a half mile to Penn Place. At Number 50, you'll find Route 66 (the shop) and a treasure trove of T-shirts, handmade jewelry, prints, and highway memorabilia.

Route 66 is always evolving. Time-honored businesses close, and some storefront merchants who now advertise themselves as trading posts have no understanding of the term. So it's a cause for some celebration when a new

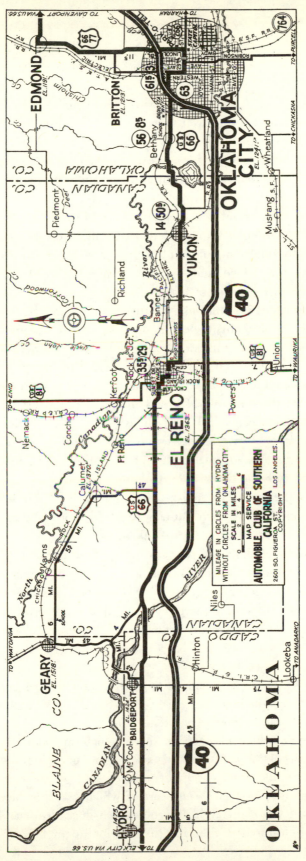

Reproduced by permission

Route 66 enterprise presents itself as just that. At the Route 66 shop you'll find an eclectic collection served up with elegance. The owner is witty, warm, and of a kindly disposition toward travelers in from the road. And that in itself is special.

So if you're looking for an exclusive item to take home from your tour of the highway, the Route 66 shop is a wonderful place to browse.

To rejoin Route 66, head west on I-44, exit at 39th (SR 66) and pass through Bethany. Continue on the four-lane to Yukon, or jog south a mile after Council Road, cross the bridge and follow the breezes along Lake Overholser's lovely north shore.

Back in 1941, this lake was the first and only body of water in Oklahoma to be officially designated as a seaplane base. Pan American Airways' graceful Clippers were all the rage then and transcontinental seaplane travel was considered to be the next major development in air travel. But by the time World War II had ended, military and civilian engineers had built thousands of miles of long concrete runways almost everywhere. The seaplane era was over, even for small craft, and Lake Overholser's hopes faded with the times.

At the far side of the lake, bear right at the Y-intersection and head west to Mustang Road. Jog north and take the four-lane westbound to **Yukon.**

Many of the main-street buildings here preserve the feeling of Route 66 towns. Yukon is also the beginning of a transition from midwest to west. From here on, roadside drawls will become more pronounced as farms give way to ranches and the real West begins. If you observe closely, you'll actually see the change taking place between here and the Texas border.

Also, should you happen to be in Yukon at day's end, check out the huge chase-light sign atop the Yukon Flour Mill. It can be positively mesmerizing.

Approaching El Reno on the old highway, watch for the Big 8 Motel, advertising itself as AMARILLO'S FINEST. And no, the owners are not confused. The sign is a legacy from the movie *Rain Man*, part of which was shot here. In fact you can stay in the room—set-dressed just as it was—featured in the film. Just ask for Room 117. You may even be checked in by the same fellow (only a little typecasting here) who played the desk clerk in the picture. Now all you need is a 1949 Buick with portholes. Or Dustin's phone number.

Dynaflowing on west, continue straight, or for the older alignment turn north on Sheppard at the signal, then curve west along the cemetery on Elm. At the water tower signal, turn north on Rock Island (US 81N). Just a few blocks along, on the right side, is the remarkable BPOE Lodge. This building was once part of an Oklahoma territorial exhibit (remember, Oklahoma was not yet a state) at the St. Louis Exposition of 1904—the fair that introduced the world to hot dogs and ice cream. Next to chili, that's about as American as you can get. When the exhibit closed, the building was disassembled and brought to El Reno as a permanent structure. If the Elks are not the Best People On Earth, as their sign suggests, they are certainly among the most industrious.

At Wade, turn west again, then north on Choctaw and west on Sunset. Continue west, then bear right just after the sign for **Fort Reno,** and short of the entrance to westbound I-40. Another quick right will take you up to Fort Reno itself. But unless a special event is planned, there is little cause to linger.

Heading west, there are two choices. You may continue due west on the 1932 alignment or turn north on an older route for **Calumet** and **Geary.** Unless you have plenty of time, the straight-west route is better. Beyond the US 270 junction, continue west, bearing northwest at the Y-intersection. Follow Spur 281 to the next Y and bear southwest. Then be ready for a treat as you approach a bridge of no fewer than thirty-eight—count 'em, thirty-eight—spans.

There are lots of roadie explanations for the number of spans here: frequent washouts, the weight of tank convoys, a steel shortage, and so on. But the truth is that each of these spans is simply as large as the highway department's early equipment could lift into place. Of course, you can stick with the tank convoy story if it works better for you. Part of traveling is taking home whatever stories you like.

From **Bridgeport,** continue west toward **Hydro.**

Take care, however, for the road has several dipsy-doodles through this section, punctuated by short, unexpected stretches of gravel. There are a couple of old, live-over gas stations along here as well, including Lucille's, still operating. But it's the road itself that is really the main attraction here. Pink, tree-shaded concrete with the innocent-looking little half curbs that were once so innovative. The trouble was that the curbs accomplished more than was intended by highway engineers.

Instead of promoting drainage, they could turn a hill face into a solid sheet of water during a hard rain—which is the only kind of rain Oklahoma seems to have. If you got between two such hills, you'd likely stay there until the weather cleared. Sometimes other folks would come slithering down to the bottom, too, making an even bigger mess.

The other thing the curbs were intended to do was to redirect errant autos back onto the roadway. The curbs managed that, too. But many cars were tossed over onto their tops in the process. Not surprising you don't see a lot of this kind of curbing anymore.

Approaching **Weatherford** on the north service road of I-40, make a quick jog south onto westbound Main Street via Washington Avenue. To the north a few blocks is Southwestern Oklahoma State University. Overlooking the town, the site is all the more attractive for its early architecture, recalling the days when it served only as a teachers' college. The campus remains one of the prettiest anywhere along the route.

The Out to Lunch Cafe on the right at midtown is a good spot if you're ready to have a light meal and regroup. You can even sign their wall. Nice folks, good food, and pretty, down-home waitresses who aren't required to babble their names and push the daily special. Here, they'll just smile that wonderful Oklahoma *Hi-y'all* smile and let you make up your own mind. Next best thing to sharing the front-porch swing and a lemonade with your sweetie.

Departing Weatherford, continue straight west as the state highway curves southwest, and turn south on 4th Street (SR 54). Follow the sharp bend west and continue on old Route 66 on the north side of I-40. Slowing for really *evil* speed bumps, cross over at the T-intersection, turn west at the stop, continuing on the southside beyond the next interchange.

Return to the north side as necessary and continue on the four-lane into **Clinton,** entering on Choctaw Avenue. Pop Hicks Restaurant stood along here, a 1936 landmark that was like a town bulletin board with silverware. It burned in 1999, with no insurance. For the city route, turn south on 4th Street, then west on Frisco Avenue. It's pure Main Street America.

Most Elvis sightings on old Route 66 have a distinct UFO quality, but you really can sleep in a room where Elvis stayed, at the Trade Winds Courtyard Inn. Or, if Elvis isn't your style, they might have a Margaret O'Brien Room. You could ask.

Leaving Clinton, there is a definite scenery-or-food choice to make. To follow old Route 66, turn south on 10th Street and continue as it becomes Neptune Drive. Bear west at the Y, to the right of the old motel and roadhouse, and head west on Commerce Road.

But if your lip is set for a world-class barbecue sandwich on a bun the size of Delaware, make tracks for the interstate and Jiggs Smokehouse. Jiggs used to advertise on a billboard along the highway, but most of the sign fell down some years ago. Didn't matter, though. The place is so well known now that customers from both coasts show up regularly for their barbecue-beef fix. Even grab-it-and-go people, who don't usually notice their food or care that much for barbecue, end up way down the highway, licking the wax paper and regretting the miles. Jiggs is on the north side of I-40 at the Parkersburg Road exit just west of Clinton. Come and set a spell.

West Commerce Road leads to the Strafford exit, where you may continue on the north service road, recrossing to the south side at Clinton Lake Road and crossing again to the north side just beyond the railroad, or head for **Elk City** on I-40. Enter Elk City on the four-lane, continuing west a mile and a half to the exit just beyond the T-33 jet. Jog west on Country Club, continuing to the park, then turn south at the church onto Main Street. Follow Main to Broadway, turn west, and continue to the T at Pioneer. Jog one block north, then turn west on Third.

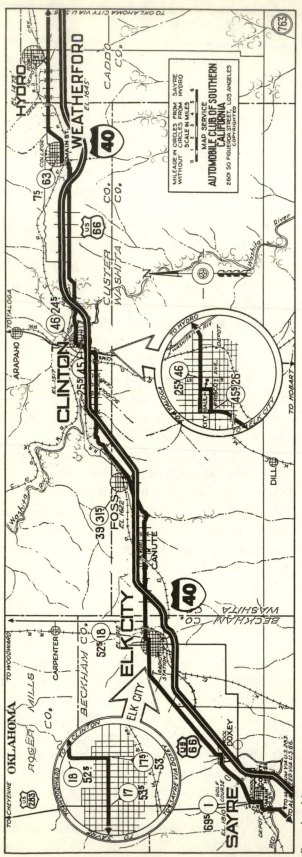

At the intersection is a museum and a pleasant park with a train ride for kids.

If it's lunchtime, however, you'll want to head back down Third to the Country Dove, a gift shop and tearoom extraordinaire. Oklahoma is not, as you may have discovered, a souper's paradise. But even if a light vegetarian lunch rings no bells for you, the French Silk pie will. This dessert is so light, it's like sampling chocolate air and will leave you wondering whether you should use a fork or just smear it right on your body.

To continue on the older alignment, jog right onto the north frontage road just before the I-40 entrance, crossing to the south side after four and a half miles, and recrossing to the north side at Cemetery Road. Continue on into **Sayre,** turning right at the stop onto Business Loop 40. Through Sayre, bear south on Fourth Street (US 283) and follow it directly across Red River (whence the movie of the same name) without jogging west on Main, where the older bridge is closed.

It was at the old Route 66 bridge in Sayre that the Great Indian Uprising of 1959 is said to have occurred. The bridge itself had burned and was barricaded. But as each out-of-state car slowed for the detour, Sayre high school students excitedly told the tourists to roll up their windows and head west as fast as possible because Indians had burned the bridge and were on the warpath. For the better part of a day, the Oklahoma Highway Patrol had its hands full stopping all the speeding cars headed for Texas—and safety from all those rampaging Indians.

Heading west at a more leisurely pace, turn onto the north frontage road a mile beyond the present bridge, crossing under I-40 to the south side and continuing west into **Erick.** This pleasant, helpful town also had a speeding problem, but it was no joke. In fact, Erick had become known as one of the worst speed traps in the nation. Using a speedy black 1938 Ford with Oklahoma overdrive, Officer Elmer could catch just about anyone he had a mind to. When he once busted Bob Hope, the comedian quipped on his next radio show that the only way he'd go through Erick again would be on a donkey.

But Officer Elmer's prowess soon proved too much for the town. Tourist business had fallen off badly, and Elmer

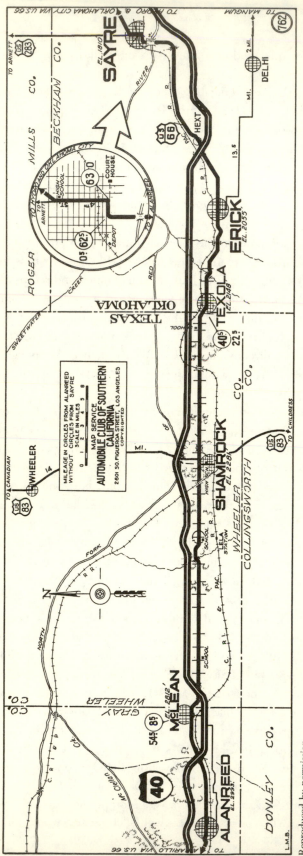

had to go—at least officially. But on dark nights, some travelers along this stretch of road say that an old black Ford V-8 still has a way of appearing suddenly in the rearview mirror. Just a warning, perhaps.

Farther down the road in **Texola,** it was a different tale. A few years before, there had been travelers and truck drivers all over the place. Never a boisterous town, folks were awakened one morning to find that some pranksters had climbed up to a huge TEXOLA sign facing onto the highway. There, they'd simply changed the T to an S. Within hours, strangers were making purchases just to ask where the house (as in *house*) was located.

There is only a foundation now where the welcoming sign with the saucy message once stood. But if you scrunch up your eyes a little, it's not hard to imagine how inviting that sign must have looked to someone long on the road and far from home.

5

TEXAS

Without a river or some continental rift, border crossings between states usually pass without notice. But not here. Almost immediately after entering Texas, the land changes. It's almost as if someone looked carefully at this place and decided, without regard for political interests, that the state line just naturally belonged right *here*.

Leaving the rolling, wooded hills of Oklahoma, the Panhandle of Texas opens like an immense natural stage. In the space of a few miles the land becomes flatter, more angular, a little threatening. Not a good place to have a horse pull up lame if you were a line-rider. Not a good place to have your clapped-out old truck throw a rod if you were an Okie family trying gamely with your little ones to reach California. Not a gentle place at all. But a place magnificent, like the sea, in its sheer, endless expanse. And in the way the land challenges you to open yourself to it, to take it all in—or scuttle quickly across to an easier region.

Few places in America scrape at primitive human emotions the way Texas does. People who live on this land are afflicted either with the fierce loyalty known only to those who have learned to hold adversity lightly in their hands, or the equally burning desire to get the hell out of here.

Even the remnant of old Route 66 has a hunkered-down look as it climbs toward the breaks just west of

Alanreed. Beyond these crumbling bluffs the high plains begin in earnest. A few miles more and the tumbled character of the land disappears almost completely, surrendering to a vast, treeless plain that flattens the entire horizon all the way into New Mexico.

Windy, dry, appearing virtually limitless, even to the 65-mile-an-hour eye, the distances seem endless:

> The sun has riz,
> The sun has set,
> And here we is
> In Texas yet.

So convinced were the earliest travelers that they were in imminent danger of simply becoming lost to death out here that they drove stakes into even the slightest rise to point the way. Coming upon these frail markers, riders from the south named this region Llano Estacado—the Staked Plain.

As you cross this land now with relative ease, imagine yourself out here alone, in an earlier time. Stakes or no, could you have walked this two-hundred-mile stretch in search of something better than you had back home? Would you have done that? Interesting to notice what a tight grasp old Demon Comfort can have on us, isn't it?

But rather than just looking through the windshield at what lies everywhere around, take a few minutes out in the open along this stretch of road, or down by Claude, or out near Adrian, beyond Amarillo. Walk for a bit, away from your car-cocoon and the certainty of a smooth, predictable highway. Even a few yards will do—toward whatever spot announces itself to you.

Get acquainted with the wind. No words, no other medium, can convey what earlier passers-through must have felt here on this land. But the wind still communicates it perfectly. So find that spot, walk out to it, and clear your mind for a few minutes. Notice what you're feeling as you stand facing into a wind older that the plain itself. Take just a moment to know something of this land before you move on. Sense what it means to be out here.

In Texas.

SHAMROCK
TO ADRIAN

Continue on the south service road from Texola, entering **Shamrock** on Business Loop 40. At the junction with US 83, be sure U Drop Inn, as the name once suggested, and you'll find a friendly spot for a coffee break. You'll also find this service station complex, dating from 1936, is one of the finest examples of art deco architecture on all of old Route 66. Shamrock, once a booming oil and gas center, celebrates its Irish heritage. But somehow the image is muddled. A leprechaun in chaps? Duke Wayne in a green derby hat?

Continuing west, it's easier to take the interstate. You'll see portions of old Route 66, particularly on the south side of I-40, but most sections are isolated or difficult to reach. **McLean** is one of the nicer towns in the Panhandle, however, so you may want to exit. Life is slower paced here. On Sunday morning, people on the way to church all take care to wave hello to a stranger. Small towns like this were once the extended families of America. McLean still is.

Like many Panhandle towns, McLean has suffered from a roller-coaster oil business (pronounced *awl bidness* in Texas) as well as being bypassed by the interstate. But townspeople are preserving McLean's ties to the old road. At the east end of town, a Sears brassière factory has become a barbed wire (pronounced *bob war*) museum with a walk-through Route 66 display. At the west end, there's a vintage Phillips 66 station and tanker truck. Farther along, you'll find the Cactus Inn, newly refurbished and ready for guests.

Departing McLean, follow the southside frontage road through **Alanreed.** A troublesome dirt section lies west of town, so it's best to rejoin I-40, exiting again on SR 70 south to Jericho. Turn west there and jog on into **Groom,** where the Golden Spread Grill has been serving travelers and locals for years. When the noon siren blows, everyone in town shows up.

Nearby, the Britten USA water tower is sure to get your attention, just as it was intended to do. How many

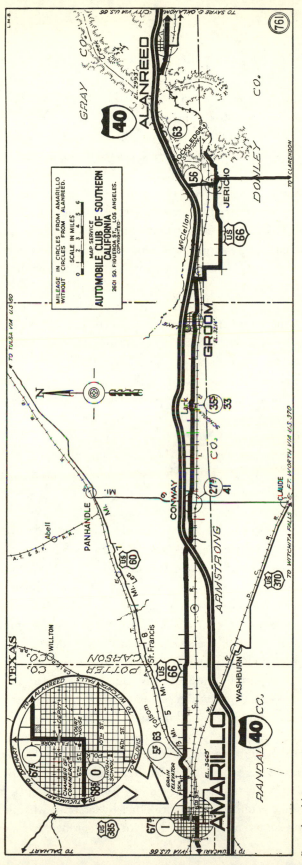

tourists do you suppose bought a little of this or that when they stopped to ask about this leaning tower of Texas? It's marketing in the best roadside tradition.

At the next I-40 junction (Exit 85), a few miles west of Conway, you'll have a choice. If you want to check out the Big Texan, a newer Route 66 tradition, continue on I-40 to Exit 75 in Amarillo.

For more advanced cases of the kind of too-flat fever this section of highway can sometimes induce, head south on I-27 and turn east at **Canyon** on SR 217. Here, less than half an hour from Amarillo, is one of the most beautiful areas to be found anywhere in the Southwest: Palo Duro Canyon.

It's as if Nature felt that the Panhandle plains needed some bit of contrast—an exception to prove the rule. If so, Palo Duro is certainly that. The colors, in haunting desert tints, and the unexpected formations of this canyon are unique. Hiking trails are well laid out, along with miles of scenic drives and bridle paths. Horses are available and there is even a miniature narrow-gauge railroad for the youngsters. The canyon is at its best early and late in the day, especially in the heat of summer, so plan ahead.

To follow Route 66 through **Amarillo,** cross to the north side of I-40 at the junction west of Conway and take Business Loop 40 into the city on Amarillo Boulevard. There is strong feeling of the old flat road along here, though it becomes a little ticky-tacky closer to town. But don't sell Amarillo short. It's one of the most underrated cities along old Route 66 and worth some time. Since part of the original route is now one-way, turn south on Pierce Street and then west again on 6th Street. This neighborhood is a great comeback story in itself. Instead of urban blight, you'll now find a mile-long stretch of successful Route 66–era businesses. Plan your strategy at a table in the Neon Cafe, then fan out to cover the delightful boutiques, antique shops and bookstores you'll find along here.

Originally, this area was part of the suburb of **San Jacinto Heights** and it still bears some of the feeling of Texas towns where the Bible Belt runs head on into the Wild West tradition. Rooming houses employing, according to one Amarillo city official, "ladies of whenever" were sometimes exorcised when the property changed hands in order to drive off whatever naughty spirits might remain. Yet while they operated, these houses sat cheek-by-hog-jowl with a family restaurant where the original Pig Hip sandwich was created in 1930.

Not too far away, the Amarillo Natatorium offered indoor swimming as at least a temporary respite from summertime heat. Truly a Panhandle phenomenon, The Nat looked like an architectural Appaloosa horse—with a graystone Moorish-Camelot front half joined to a porthole-dotted steamship posterior. Although the pool concept didn't pan out, The Nat did become an outstanding attraction as a ballroom. Reopening in 1926 (the same year in which Route 66 was chartered), The Nat hosted the top bands of the '30s and '40s—Paul Whiteman, Count Basie, Louis Armstrong, Benny Goodman, and Harry James. Not bad for a former swimming hole.

But West 6th Street is probably best remembered for its Texas-style, shoot-from-the-hip marketing. During hard times, one grocer took to announcing his daily specials to shoppers from the rooftop of his building. And the way he got the crowd's attention was by tossing live chickens off the roof. Now, while it's a fact that chickens in their natural state can do a little flying, these were market-ready, clipped-wing models with all the flight characteristics of a feathered rock. From the roof, about the best anyone could expect was a barely controlled free-fall. So, if you were headed for this grocery, you had to be prepared. And you probably had to like chicken a lot.

The Chicken Follies are gone now—and just as well—but you'll find much of interest before leaving this part of Amarillo. Jogging southwest on Bushland and then west on 9th Avenue, continue on out of town. West of Amarillo, old Route 66 exists only as the north service road for I-40, just a few yards away, so there is little advantage in taking the old road with its frequent stop signs and careless pick-up trucks.

West of Amarillo, on the south side via Exit 62, keep watch for a row of ten Cadillacs—in various stages of fin—augered methodically into the land just south of the interstate. Although it looks as if it could have been left by Druids, Cadillac Ranch was in fact placed here by pop-art financier Stanley Marsh, 3. It may also be the clearest visual statement ever about wretched excess in oil-propelled America. Try as we will to ignore the message of these iron dinosaurs, we cannot. *Change your ways,* they say in mute eloquence, *or join us.*

Out by **Vega,** both the Best Western Sands and the Comfort Inn are pleasant motels away from the city. Or if staying in authentic places along the old highway warms your heart, try the Vega Motel. It's a very clean original, including those old in-between garages, plus furnishings from the 1940s. On Route 66 at US 385.

Along this section, keep an eye out for the MidPoint water tower in **Adrian.** Based on averages from the Chiago—Los Angeles Mileage Table in the back of this guide, Adrian is the geo-mathematical center of old Route 66 as you've been driving it.

So throw yourself a little celebration at the MidPoint Cafe. It's a friendly place featuring good food nicely served. In addition to the adjoining antique shop, the cafe features furnishings from a period drugstore. What's more, it's all for sale. Say *Ha*—that's Texan for *Hi*—when you mosey in. Say hello to Fran, the owner, and be sure to ask for a free MidPoint bumper sticker. As the locals will tell you: *When you're here, you're halfway there.*

Beyond Adrian the old road continues for only a few miles, then you'll be rejoining I-40 until you reach the Glenrio exit on the New Mexico border.

6

NEW MEXICO

New Mexico is descended from the sky. Other places along old Route 66 have been formed from rivers, mountains, and plains. Other states have been forged by iron-willed men meeting in urgency behind closed doors to make a truce, a compromise, a set of defensible boundaries. But New Mexico has no door on its history, no roof on its being. The first allegiance of most people here is to the land and to the generous sky above. Boundaries here seem best determined where these two—earth and sky—meet.

In the New Mexican view, cities are to be used as gathering points—for art as much as commerce—and not for population centers or power bases. Santa Fe is older than any city of Colonial America, and has been a capital for more than three hundred years, yet its population barely tops 75,000. The oldest public building in the United States is here in Santa Fe. Yet even with such a head start, the city refuses to have a proper airport. Newcomers rarely understand this until they have lived here for a while. Then they realize why there is no major airline operation in Santa Fe. . . . It would interfere with the sky.

In New Mexico, travelers along old Route 66 begin to notice something different in the sky above about the time they reach Tucumcari. The color—a deeper, more translucent lens of cobalt blue—can take even experienced color photographers by surprise. No wonder the painters, and after them the writers, began migrating here well before Route

66 first made its way across the state. Driving through New Mexico's high country in crackling bright sunshine, or rolling through one of the long valleys with billowing rain clouds so close overhead they seem almost touchable, everything here seems to put you at stage center. You always seem to be right in the middle of the performance.

It's easy for a traveler to get religion—any kind—in a place like New Mexico, where earth and sky and wind and water greet one another in such unexpected ways. All the simple distinctions of mind, former notions about what is and what isn't, begin to blur. Following old Route 66 at a slower pace through the eastern hills, across the Continental Divide and into serious mesa country, perceptions change. It's easier here, as an observer, to become part of all that is being observed, to feel a sense of connection with everything around. As a traveler, it is easier to slip loose from the sense of detachment and not-belonging that often seems to be a part of any great crossing.

This enchanted land asks little of you as a traveler, except one thing. It asks that you allow yourself to become enchanted, too.

GLENRIO TO ALBUQUERQUE

Although the sign for a business loop through **Glenrio** may be somewhat misleading, this nearly empty town remains one of the most charming vestiges along old Route 66. The well-known Last Motel in Texas/First Motel in Texas flourished just east of the state line. But its sign has faded and fallen, along with the hopes and dreams of another bypassed town. The old route does continue on into **San Jon,** but if you wish to visit there, check on the old road, which may be covered over with slippery gravel, and consider rejoining the interstate for a few miles. Then, at San Jon, return to the old road on the south side and continue west toward **Tucumcari,** crossing to the north side just before town.

For most old Route 66 travelers, the *real* West began with some simple but meaningful event. For some it was

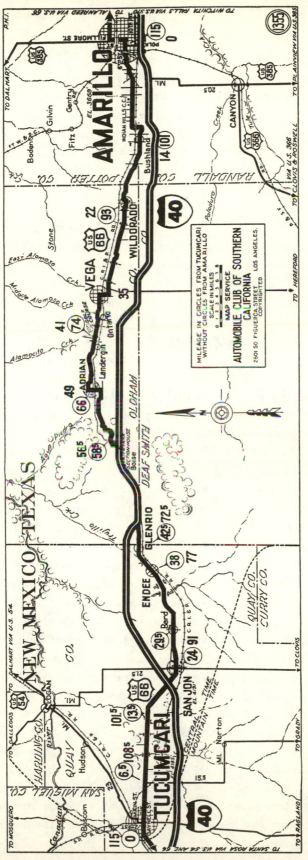

the first glimpse of the long, low, fencelike sign for Whiting
Brothers. For others, it was arriving in Tucumcari. City
of 2,000 rooms. The only place to spend tonight. With
powerful roadside advertising it was tough to pass Tucumcari by, and few did. Following Business Loop 40
(Gaynell Street on the accompanying map), you'll see many
survivors: The Tee Pee, Blue Swallow, Palomino. Sweet
reminders, still among us.

Heading west, road conditions require that you return
to I-40 through the stretch from **Montoya** through
Newkirk to **Cuervo**—three dear but near-death towns,
strung out along old Route 66 like amulets on an antique
Spanish chain.

This is part of a very old route, the first New Mexico
road begun with federal aid, back in 1918. The tiny grocery
stores were not only tourist stops but the center of life
here, connecting travelers, townspeople, and those who
have always roamed these barrancas. Richardson's Store
& Good Gulf, Knowles Grocery, Wilkerson's, all way stations for regular long-haul rigs, touring cars, ponies, and
daily school buses. Hanging on, hoping for a Route 66
revival. But like the hand-painted signs on the old clap-
board siding, fading fast.

From Cuervo the interstate is easiest. But the original
alignment can be followed over a short unimproved stretch
south to SR 156, then east over pavement to US 84. This
is a wonderful stretch of the old two-lane with much of
the feel of Route 66 across New Mexico during the 1930s
and 1940s—open, free of commercial development, and
wild. Especially wild. After turning west onto SR 156,
you'll notice the small animals and birds by the thousands
inhabiting the ground cover lining both edges of the highway. So please, if you intend to drive this section, don't
exceed 45 miles per hour. Many creature-generations have
passed since these roadside inhabitants were traffic-wise.
And they are part of what makes this segment of Route
66 special. Give them the benefit of your choice to drive
this section with extra care.

Continue west on SR 156, then jog north on US 84, passing under I-40 to enter **Santa Rosa** on Will Rogers Drive.
Santa Rosa is also a Route 66 landmark. But unlike Tucumcari, needed far less advertising. Santa Rosa has the weather.

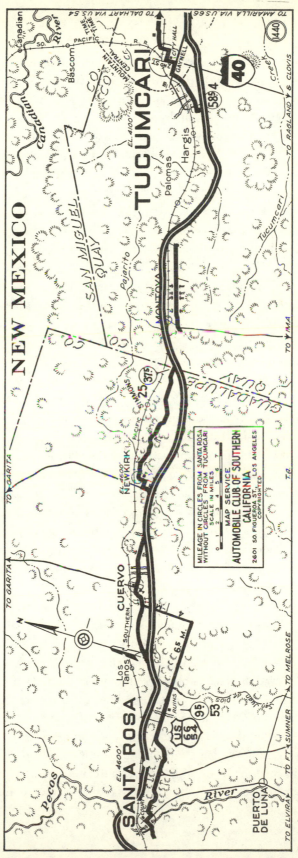

More people have been snowbound in Santa Rosa than anywhere west of St. Louis. And it's a pretty good place to be stranded. For years, it was the home of the Club Cafe, known for its biscuits and gravy as well as the satisfied-looking Fat Man on billboards along Route 66.

The Club Cafe finally closed. But its spirit—along with the famous logo—has been preserved and enriched by the family-owners of Joseph's Bar & Grill, right on the route at 865. Live bands on weekends. Always good food with great care for travelers. Snowing or not, be sure to stop in.

If Santa Fe is your preference, turn north on US 84 west of Santa Rosa, which joins the old Route 66 alignment to the north near **Dilia** and continue on to **Romeroville.** From there, turn southwest to follow Route 66, also known as Las Vegas Highway, along a 46-mile loop swinging northwest to **Pecos.** Continuing southwest on SR 50, you must rejoin I-25 briefly.

Take Exit 294 at Cañoncito to rejoin the route north on Pecos Trail. **Santa Fe** is unique, so plan to spend some time here. There are so many fine restaurants and galleries, you could easily eat and art yourself into oblivion.

Pepper's Restaurant and Cantina, in the Pecos Trail Inn at 2209 Old Pecos Trail is a good place to begin. After the road becomes Old Santa Fe Trail (shown as College Street on the map inset) and you approach the Plaza, watch for the Old Santa Fe Trail Bookstore and Bistro at Number 613. Closer in, at 406 Old Santa Fe Trail, the Pink Adobe Dragon Room offers live trees growing up through the dining area and southwest cuisine with a Cajun touch.

Jog west on Water Street and then north again to the Plaza, the epicenter of Santa Fe style—all of which comes at a price, however, with downtown accommodations easily topping $200 per night. Fortunately, El Rey Inn, at 1862 Cerrillos Road is on the outbound route and offers ambiance from the '30s at moderate rates, with charming fireplace rooms and a continental breakfast.

Departing the Plaza west, turn south on Don Gaspar, jog west on De Vargas, and continue south on Galisteo to Cerrillos. Hungry again? Good, because a mile before El Rey Inn in Tecolote, at 1203 Cerrillos, featuring down-home

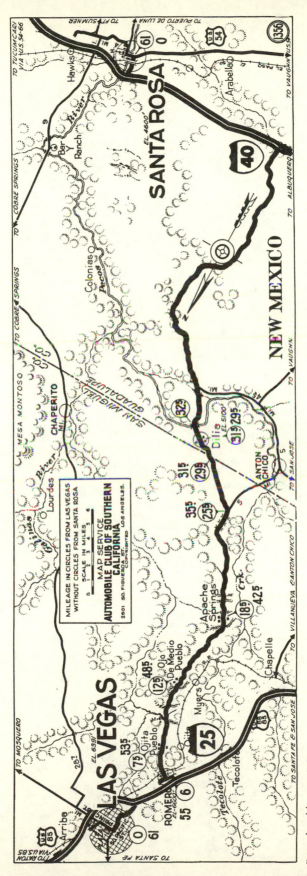

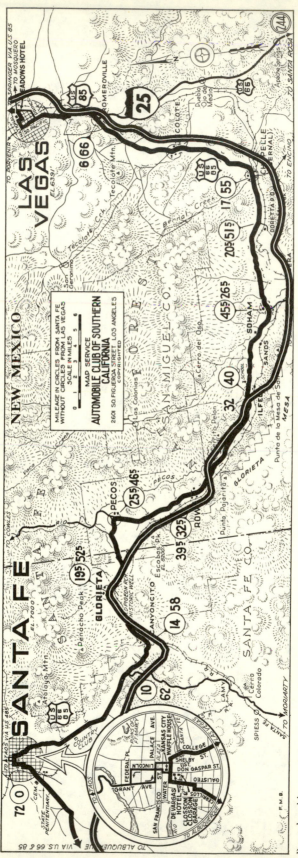

Reproduced by permission

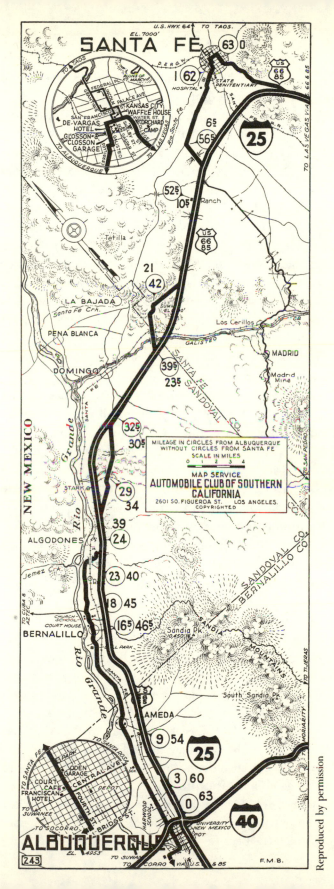

huevos rancheros and a clientele to match. And if you're in a Steinbeck frame of mind, there's Tortilla.

Continue south on I-25, about halfway to **Algodones,** to a tiny bit of another world and as remarkable a place as you're likely to find. It's the Santo Domingo Indian Trading Post, a couple of miles west of the interstate. Half hidden in a stand of cottonwood trees, wedged in between Galisteo Creek and the railroad tracks near **Domingo,** Fred Thompson's place is one of a kind. *Life* magazine once came here to do a piece. And his curiosity aroused, President Kennedy turned up here in 1962. You can buy nearly anything but the old Frazer sedan that has been sitting out front for thirty years. How about a few postcards and a soda? Some Dr. McLean's Volcanic Liniment? You also might check the names in the 5,000-page guest register—it's even money that some neighbor of yours once visited here, too.

Continuing south on I-25, take the Algodones exit for the old route (SR 313) through **Bernalillo** and **Alameda.** Nearing Albuquerque, the road becomes SR 556 and 4th Street. Follow 4th to Bridge Boulevard, jog west for the Barelas Bridge, and south again on Isleta Boulevard (SR 314). Turn west on SR 6 to **Los Lunas** and continue to the junction with I-40 at **Correo.** This route, with everything from near-zero traffic density to a row of baby volcanoes, also offers an occasional glimpse of old, old, old Route 66 to the south. Whether you've been following the interstate or the old road, SR 6 from Albuquerque and Los Lunas to Correo (Suwanee) is a fine section.

Meantime, if you've chosen the direct route to Albuquerque via Clines Corners, Moriarty, and Tijeras, just continue west from Santa Rosa on I-40. But take a moment for Longhorn Ranch at Exit 203. Although not typical of early mom-and-pop attractions, the Longhorn does sport some of the carnival feeling of the old route.

Returning to the interstate, continue to the **Moriarty** exit and follow the old route through town. From Tijeras follow the old alignment, now marked SR 333, through the pass and into **Albuquerque.**

Both the old highway and the newer interstate look easily laid out through this area, but that is part of the road builder's art. Because Tijeras Canyon was such tough

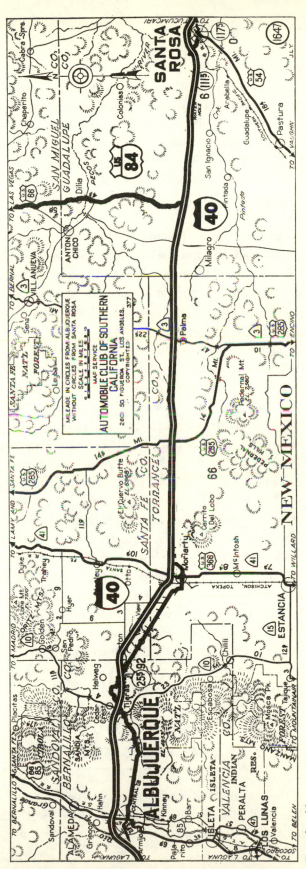

going, new construction has often been delayed on this section. Consider a report from the New Mexico Highway Department from as late as 1951. It described the result of setting off dynamite charges in a thousand holes that had been laboriously drilled in one small area. That's a *thousand* charges set off simultaneously. A big bang, all right. But here's the clincher. After all that, there was so little debris that it took only twenty minutes to clear it all up.

If you've stayed on the interstate, you can exit for the business loop at Central Avenue. However, there is very little feeling of old Route 66 along the eastern reaches of Central Avenue. A route that leaves more time for touring the downtown section is to exit at San Mateo Avenue (SR 367) southbound and turn west again on Central. Local revitalization projects have done wonders in preserving and maintaining charming shops and businesses in the downtown area. The 66 Diner at 1405 Central Avenue is a fine nouveau-'50s eatery. And Lindy's has been serving terrific chili and other excellent fare since 1929. Newly renovated, Lindy's is a family-owned tradition open 24 hours on Central at Fifth Street to serve hungry roadies anytime.

Motel properties have fared less well, though a few survivors like the De Anza and El Vado are well kept. But for a truly special stay, La Posada, a block north of Central at 125 Second Street, has been lovingly restored and is the choice for romantic charm from bygone days. A concert grand piano accompanies afternoon happy hour and the coffee shop is a 1930s classic and first-rate. Enjoy.

Another of Albuquerque's restorations is the lovely KiMo Theater, past the center of town. Originally built by the Boller Brothers, recognized in the Southwest for their Hi-Ho Rococo style, it now stands as a model of what can and should be accomplished all along old Route 66.

ALBUQUERQUE
TO MANUELITO

After crossing the Old Town Bridge westbound, continue up Nine-Mile Hill, so called because its crest is exactly that distance from Albuquerque's center. If it's early morning or

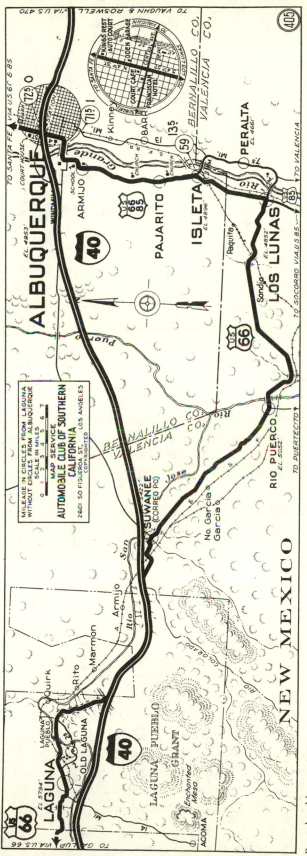

evening, or if there are clouds over the Sandia Mountains to the east, it's worth a photo stop near the top of the hill.

For I-40 travelers, there's a special treat ahead. At **Mesita** (Exit 117), turn left and double back toward the interstate to follow the old two-lane west into Laguna. Mesas, cottonwoods, sweet curving roadway—these few miles are some of the most beautiful anywhere, and are best driven at a slow pace. Also, keep watch for children playing and people walking along the road. This is reservation land and we are guests here.

Continuing west on the interstate, take the **Laguna** (SR 124) exit for a superb section of old Route 66. This stretch of road is a little slower than SR 6 from Los Lunas, but has more feeling of the Southwest during the 1930s and '40s than nearly any other part of the old route. There's also much to be rediscovered here, so take your time. At the Laguna Pueblo, jog south to follow the older alignment until it returns to the four-lane. This little loop, especially, is like driving right into an old View-Master scene.

Approaching **Budville,** bear north with the old alignment, which passes through **Cubero** and returns. It was at nearby Villa Cubero that Ernest Hemingway settled in with his notebooks to write a major part of *The Old Man and the Sea*. He knew as well as anyone that the quality of human perception depends on contrast. If you are going to write about something like the sea, one way to hold the vision of that sea in stark relief is to go as far from it as you can. Cubero filled the bill.

Crossing to the south side of I-40 from Cubero, the old route continues past **McCartys.** A little farther on it recrosses to the north side, SR 124 ends, and you'll rejoin I-40 to the **Grants** exit. If you're among the many who are traveling in summer, you may want to head south from Grants to the perpetual Ice Caves, where the temperature never rises above 31°F. Even if you've already done some caving, you'll find this attraction to be different. From Grants, the old road continues as SR 122 through **Milan, Prewitt,** and **Thoreau** (pronounced locally as *Threw*) and across the Continental Divide. Return to I-40 for just over ten miles, then take the Iyanbito Exit and continue into **Gallup** on the main thoroughfare, marked Highway 66.

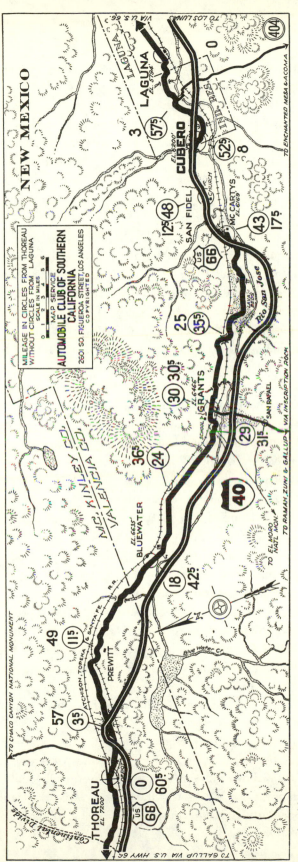

NEW MEXICO

MAP SERVICE
AUTOMOBILE CLUB OF SOUTHERN CALIFORNIA
MILEAGE IN CIRCLES FROM THOREAU
WITHOUT CIRCLES FROM LAGUNA
SCALE IN MILES
0 1 2 3 4 5 6
2601 SO. FIGUEROA STREET, LOS ANGELES
COPYRIGHTED

More than most cities on the highway, Gallup maintains a sense of the Route 66 era. Little has been lost and, as the old alignment jogs south on First Street, then west on Coal Avenue before returning to Highway 66, look for some of the fine old buildings like the Drake and Grand hotels, and the El Morro Theater, also designed by the Boller Brothers. Ask for the guide to historic buildings when you arrive.

Gallup also has something few other places on Route 66 can claim—a longtime Hollywood connection. From *Redskin*, filmed in 1929, to the more recent adventures of *Superman*, the Gallup area has provided unequaled movie scenery. And El Rancho Hotel, now beautifully and responsibly restored, was the on-location home to stars like Tracy and Hepburn, Bogart, Hayworth, Flynn, and Peck. A production designer's dream, the hotel at first looks like an architectural collision between Mount Vernon and a backlot set for *Viva Villa*. There's even an Uncle Remus Wishing Well out front. Still, the overall effect is both inviting and absolutely right. How could it be otherwise? El Rancho, it has always been said, was designed for none other than R. E. Griffith, brother of the great film pioneer D. W. Griffith.

But hold the phone! There's a mystery brewing here. Exactly the kind of tale that the stars who stayed here, and movie fans everywhere, love. The truth is, D. W. Griffith *never had* a brother named R. E. Griffith. Those initials appear to belong instead to Raymond E. Griffith, a silent-film star turned comedy writer and producer.

R.E. had talent, no doubt about that, and was a production whiz, but he had another characteristic, too. He was known in the industry as a pathological teller of tales, often making up outlandish stories just to see if he could get away with it.

Or the obscure Mr. Griffith may have been another person altogether. But whatever his true identity, you've got to give the fellow credit. He put his D. W. Griffith story over on everyone for fifty years. So when you stay at El Rancho—and you simply must—drop by the tap room and hoist a glass to the memory of R. E. Griffith, who in death as in life damn near did fool all of the people all of the time.

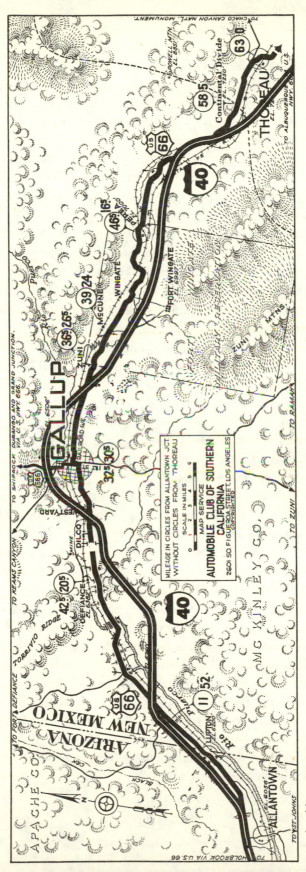

Reproduced by permission

Gallup remains one of the great cultural centers of New Mexico, so keep watch for some remarkable outdoor sculptures on the right, like "Bebop," which commemorates Route 66 and its neon, and the giant pottery bowl, with authentic Acoma paintings.

Also on the right, midway through town, is the Southwest Cultural Center, located on the second floor of the Santa Fe Railway depot, built in 1926. In addition to the walk-through displays of the center, you'll also find a charming deli restaurant reminiscent of the El Navajo, a well-known Fred Harvey hotel sited here. The food is good and a player piano is on hand to entertain you. During the summer, there are also nightly Indian Dance Performances in a small amphitheater right next door. The shows are both exciting and free.

The Santa Fe Railway and Route 66 are intimately entwined from Albuquerque west, so if you're a rail fan the Rex Museum, farther along, with its railroad and mining displays, will have extra meaning for you.

Continue on Route 66, following SR 118 west past Fort Yellowhorse, which looks a lot like a movie set because that's what it was, having been built for the 1950 Kirk Douglas film, *The Big Carnival*.

With your camera ready to capture the murals at the ruins of Ortega's Trading Post in Lupton, continue on through **Manuelito** toward the Arizona line. For years a great arch, supported by Eiffel Towerish strap-iron columns and topped by a large US 66 shield, stood on the state border, wishing travelers well and asking them to come again. Like so many other simple things etched sharply in the common memory, the arch is gone now. Hardly even a photograph remains. But would it not be grand to create and preserve for all those who will yet travel this road a new archway in the same style? There is a sign at the border, of course. But you pass *through* an arch and only go *by* a sign. It's a different feeling, passing under an arch—a feeling far more in tune with this old road and the way it conveys us, more gently somehow, from one state to the next.

7
ARIZONA

Arizona is one of the youngest states in the Union, last of the continental territories to be admitted, and one of the most thinly populated. But Arizona can take care of itself, thank you very much.

That's the view of many folks along the route through the upper part of the state. It's been a useful attitude to have around here, too. Poor relation to the sprawling developments of southern Arizona (itself too often a poor cousin to Southern California), the northern part of the state has learned to light its own lamp, carry its own bucket.

A lot of folks living close by old Route 66 are transplants from other orphan regions—the Ozarks of Missouri or the panhandles of Oklahoma and Texas—and they know how the government-and-commerce game works: *If you want to play ball, take the sprawl and all.* Nothing doing, the people of northern Arizona have replied. Good for them.

This is harsh but beautiful country, the air clear and sharp, unspoiled for the most part. Mountains like the San Francisco Peaks rise spectacularly from a flattened landscape, allowing you to watch them come closer for hours before the highway finally curves around their base near the junction with the main north-south road.

Cattle are raised in northern Arizona, but it is not feed-and-ship cattle country so much as it is the true Cowboy-and-Indian country of western legend. Zane Grey loved this land. He rode it and walked it and wrote about it. His was a special brand of romantic western—the kind where the hero still triumphs and rides through purple sage into a crimson sunset with his equally tough but tender sweet-heart. Over the years, nearly a hundred and fifty million copies of Grey's books have been sold, with many made and remade into movies as well. So it is difficult to exagger-ate the influence his notions of manhood, womanhood, and social justice have had on the American culture, and on anyone traveling old Route 66 across this land.

What's more, with the passage of only fifty years or so, the frontier is still very much a part of everything you'll find here. Stories of shoot-outs, lost gold mines, and desert massacres are still told by the people who lived through those days. It's a time warp worth stepping into.

There is also a compelling intimacy about the way old Route 66 and the land go on together. At night, especially, there is a personal feeling of timelessness here. Once you are away from the lights—east of Holbrook, up toward the Grand Canyon, or along the great northering loop west of Seligman—take time to stand for a while in the night. Pull the darkness around you like a cloak and feel what it is to be on the frontier of your own being, the land spilling away beyond your sight and hearing. Haul the stars down—so many here you may not even recognize old friends among them. Bring them close. Feel your own breathing and the life, unseen but sensed, everywhere around.

There are not many places left in which to take a moment like this. Arizona, along old Route 66, is one of the last.

LUPTON TO FLAGSTAFF

Continuing on the south side of I-40, the old route passes through **Lupton,** on the border, and then recrosses to the north side for **Allentown, Houck, Sanders,** and **Chambers.** From Sanders to Chambers, the road on the north side is only partially paved with some gravel stretches

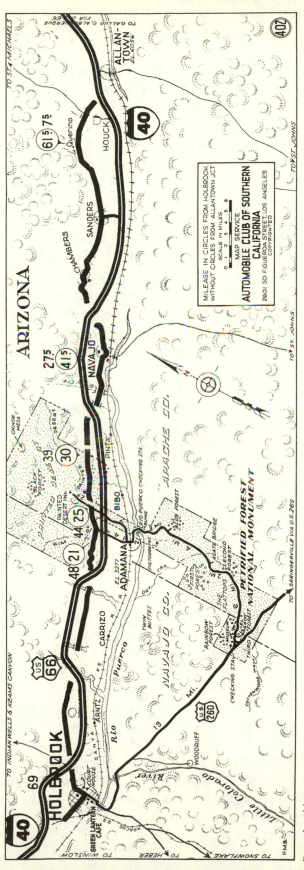

and dead ends. Since the road largely disappears most of the way from Chambers to **Holbrook,** it is better to rejoin the interstate at Lupton.

Mostly, this is a section of lost towns: Houck, Cuerino, Navapache, and Goodwater. But about twenty miles beyond Chambers, keep watch for the Petrified Forest National Park and Painted Desert. Of these, the Petrified Forest is the more interesting, with a good deal of old Route 66 flavor remaining. Take Exit 311 and cross over I-40 southbound on the Park road, then continue westbound on US 180 (formerly US 260) into Holbrook on Hopi Boulevard, following Business Loop 40.

Watch for the Pow Wow Trading Post (really a wow with the neon lit up at night), plus Joe and Aggie's Cafe. If you've always wanted to sleep in a teepee ("Oh, puh-*leeze*, can't we?"), Holbrook is the best place in the West to do it. The design for Wigwam Village was patented in 1936, with the first units constructed in Kentucky and the Southeast. A similar teepee motel was also built on old Route 66 in Rialto, California, but only the Holbrook units have been completely renovated. Call ahead, though; the Holbrook wigwams are popular.

Rejoin the interstate west of Holbrook. This was once a fairly touristy stretch of old Route 66 and some remnants like Geronimo's Trading Post still survive. Maybe you can skip the sand paintings, but can you really go home without a rubber tomahawk? There were some fine souvenir places on the old alignment through **Joseph City,** west of Business Loop 40, but these are empty or in ruin now. The Jackrabbit Trading Post hangs in there, though. All those yellow-and-black signs with the crouching rabbit that you've been seeing . . . Well, HERE IT IS!

The Jackrabbit is certainly worth a stop. It has a good feeling and the inventory is right out of the 1940s. Continuing on I-40 toward Winslow, keep watch for Hibbard Road (Exit 264). It's the beginning of a marvelous little section of old, old Route 66. Marching bravely off into the surrounding desert with its solitary line of graying telephone poles, this remnant was the first in Arizona to be bypassed when the interstate was opened here in 1958. Sadly, a bridge has now been taken out and you cannot go far.

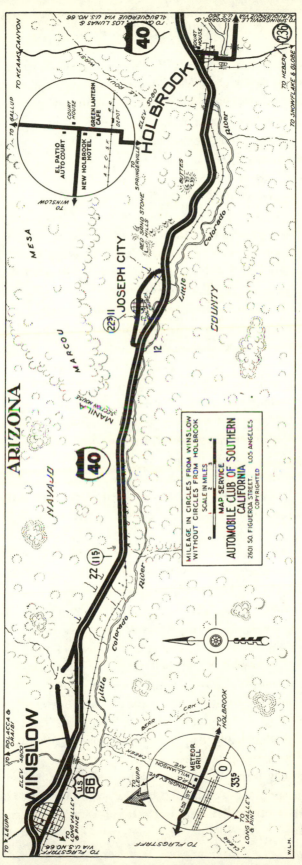

Creviced arroyos, long sloping rifts, grassy hardpan all around. This western New Mexico–eastern Arizona region has a high-desert sweetness that can make you lightheaded with solitude. Sometimes, toward either end of a long driving day, a run through this country brings up an ancient German word, *Fernweh*. It has no equivalent in English, but it represents a longing for, a need to return to, a place you've never been.

It's in the nature of a desert to be harsh. But here, on this old, old section of Route 66, there is a sense of poignance as well. If you've got a cassette player and a traveling tape collection, pull out a few tunes that bring you other voices, other times—that may even remind you of loves now gone separate ways—because this border region is special. Whether you are ambling along on the old road or slipping down the interstate, it's a stretch where you can see yourself more clearly, hear the past more sweetly.

Continuing on into **Winslow,** just follow Business Loop 40. Second Street is the best-remembered of the older alignments, but after the one-way division, both current routes become part of US 66.

Winslow is often remembered for two things: national roadside marketing and interesting ladies. Roadies often improved their prospects locally by getting duded up a bit at the Store For Men before standing on a corner to wait for a girl (my lord) in a flatbed Ford. Eagles are nothing, you see, if not observant.

Like Meramec Caverns and Jackrabbit, Winslow's Store For Men was one of the pioneers in roadside advertising. Its sign wound up as far away as Paris and Guam. And Store For Men was one of the rule-breakers, too. It was generally believed that billboards and bumper stickers might bring in travelers the first time but would not generate many return visits. Roadside ads were considered one-shots. But the Jackrabbit and Store For Men signs— which almost always appeared together—practically wallowed in repeat business.

Much of the renewed interest in old Route 66 through Winslow comes from the Old Trails Museum, just north of the route at 212 Kinsley, featuring very knowledgeable people, good exhibits, and memorabilia items like their

"Standin' on the Corner" T-shirts. The museum led a movement to restore La Posada, a former Fred Harvey hotel which has now reopened and is highly recommended.

There are a couple of very nice restaurants in Winslow, too. On the east end, at the 1100 block between the eastbound and westbound routes, is the Falcon Restaurant. The owner has been serving good food and caring for travelers on Route 66 for almost forty years. At 113 Second Street is the Whole Enchilada, a Mexican-style restaurant now connected to R.M. Bruchman's, a western tradition and a fine source for Indian curios of value since 1903.

Rejoin I-40 for the run to meteor country. Around 50,000 years ago, long before our most civilized ancestors began painting themselves blue, a giant meteorite slammed into the desert. Over the years its crater has been a prime Route 66 curiosity. Meteor City comes first at Exit 239. A descendant from an old-time trading post, the place took on the space-age look of American attractions in the 1950s.

Today, Meteor City offers a wide variety of moccasins and Indian goods along with a supply of roadside stories. The crater itself is just on down the road. There, a museum with 5,000 meteorites on display, was once housed. And the ruins of that structure, along with the famous observation tower, are still visible.

Now make a beeline for **Flagstaff.** There's plenty to see and do in this old lumbering center and university town. Great neon along motel row at night, too. Be sure to take Bobby Troup's advice, though, and "don't forget **Winona.**" It's only a one-blink town, but the folks at the little trading post are friendly and helpful. It's also the gateway to a beautiful drive along the old alignment into Flagstaff. Take the Camp Townsend/Winona Road exit, continue to the junction with US 89, and turn south into town. Route 66 is marked as such in Flagstaff, though some maps may still show it as Santa Fe Avenue.

Whatever your nightlife has been, head for the Museum Club at 4304 East Route 66, a great place to scoot your boots and soak up some honky-tonk history. *Country America* named it the top dance club, and you can still hear echoes of stars like Willie Nelson and Waylon Jennings, who played here. The owner is an avid Route 66 fan and preservationist, and the National Register of Historic Places

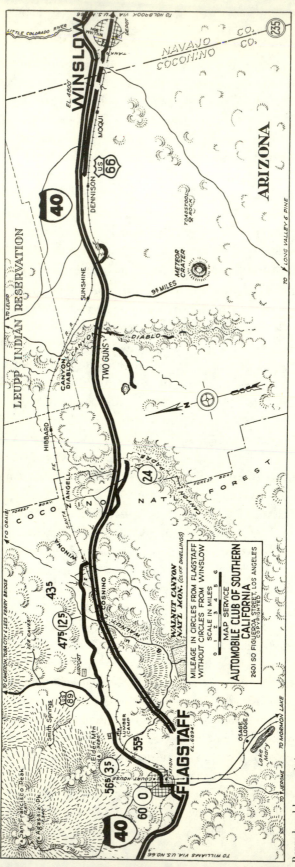

Reproduced by permission

has recently listed the Museum Club. The HoJo Inn next door is an inexpensive overnight spot, or try the very nice Best Western Woodlands Plaza on the other end of town, at 1175 West Route 66.

If you're planning a side trip to the Grand Canyon, you may wish to turn north on US 89 instead. Of the routes to either the South or North Rim, the drive north on US 89 and west on SR 64 is perhaps the most interesting. Or, if you prefer to duck into Flagstaff first, take US 180 north to **Grand Canyon Village.** When at the South Rim, it's well worth while to stay or at least take a meal at El Tovar, a grand old lodge at the canyon's edge that speaks eloquently of days gone by. With Hopi House next door, the whole place smacks of oatmeal for breakfast and daily constitutionals. It's bully. Plan well in advance, however; reservations can be difficult the year around.

If you will not be visiting Grand Canyon this time, but still have a day to spend in the area, there's a wonderful loop to the southwest through Oak Creek Canyon and **Sedona** on US 89A. Then, jogging south on SR 179, take a couple of hours at the unusual cliff dwelling of Montezuma's Castle, an early Route 66 attraction still little changed. From **Camp Verde,** return to US 89 via **Cottonwood.** Continue west and north through Chino Valley to I-40 just east of **Ash Fork.** In any case, by taking US 89 north or US 89A south, you will miss only a very little of the old alignment.

Flagstaff is a mixed bag of old Route 66 survivors and new construction, yet its motel row and businesses retain much of the old-road feeling—like the Santa Fe freights that grumble and growl just across the highway.

If you'd like to tour this charming town and are tired of following directions, catch the Flagstaff (motor) Trolley to old town, shops, restaurants, and museums. It's a nice ride and a great bargain—ride all day for under five bucks.

To continue west on Route 66, turn south onto Beaver Street one block beyond the old railroad depot, west again on Phoenix Avenue, then south on Milton Road (US 89).

now look if Flagstaff had become the movie capital of the world. Because it almost did. A few years before Route 66 began service, a talented and extremely ambitious young man was steaming west on the Atchison, Topeka & Santa Fe. Folded in his coat pocket was a new screenplay, and

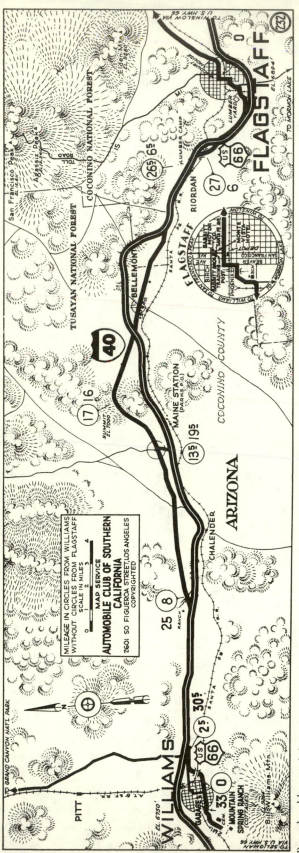

Reproduced by permission

in his mind's eye he could see every detail of how it would be made—in the real West, with real cowboys and Indians, under open skies. Fed up with Long Island studios where no one knew a cactus from a tin can, the young man was certain from his readings of Zane Grey that Flagstaff was the perfect location. The film he would make there would be grand, sweeping, magnificent—an *epic*.

It would also be wet, if he tried to make it in Flagstaff, where great, sodden flakes of snow were plopping softly into streams of icy mush along the platform as the train pulled in. For young Cecil B. DeMille, though, one look was enough. He never even left his Pullman, but went right on to Los Angeles, where he made the world's first feature-length film, *Squaw Man* (1914), using regular drugstore cowboys. But the incident must have left its mark on him, for through the monumental, biblical films DeMille later made, there always ran a theme of uncontrollable natural forces. And water, lots and lots of water.

FLAGSTAFF
TO NEEDLES

Continue west on I-40. There is a short segment of old highway on the south side at **Bellemont.** This town has a photogenic ghost-town look, but take care not to intrude on the few residents. Follow the two-lane to the north side of I-40 (or take Exit 178 farther on) for an absolutely stunning drive through the national forest on original 1930s concrete. Then at Deer Farm Road, rejoin the interstate. Business loops follow the old route through **Williams.** A pair of very interesting tours (one for mountain bikes) has been developed by the US Forest Service covering sections of nearby Route 66 now on the National Register. True roadies will want to pick up a brochure at the Chalender District office in Williams.

The long loop of old Route 66 to the California border begins at the Crookton Road exit from I-40 near **Ashfork.** Old, old roadbed is visible along this really wonderful stretch, and there's a special intimacy with the land here. **Seligman,** once a time-zone division point and now a home for goofy cars, is next. The Sno-Cap and Copper

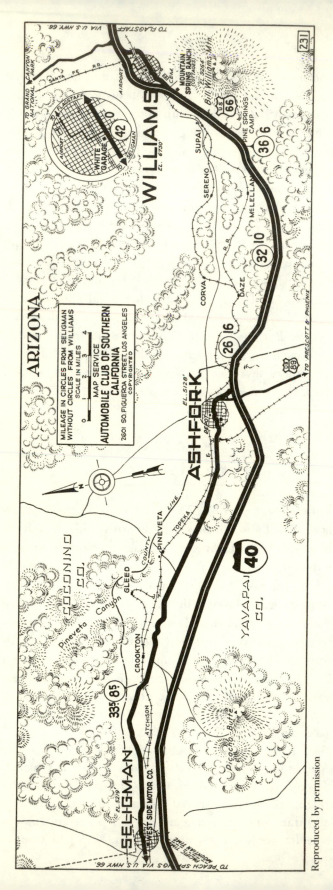

Cart are long-time Route 66 eateries, and the Seligman Barber Shop is the source of Arizona's movement to preserve the old highway.

Farther along, you'll find the Grand Canyon Caverns, perhaps the only attraction in the West to survive at such a distance from any interstate exit. Then it's on to **Peach Springs** and Crozier Canyon, where the last unpaved section of Route 66 in Arizona remained until 1937. At **Truxton,** try the Frontier Cafe. The coffee's good, the food is some of the best anywhere along the route—and the stories are on the house.

And if you think the ideals and style of the '60s in America are dead, you'll find a special treat in **Hackberry.** On the site of the old general store, a Route 66 Visitors Center has been established by one of the highway's dearest friends. Do take time to visit.

Finally, down a twenty-mile straight, **Kingman** comes into sight. After sundown, it's like being on a long final approach—more like landing than driving into town. Along Andy Devine Avenue, there are a few survivors like El Trovatore, and the Brandin' Iron Motel with a flickering neon sign that usually reads BRA IN. Farther down this winding stretch into town is a great retro-attraction, so don't linger long. Midway through Kingman at 105 E. Andy Devine, is Mr. D'z Diner. On the site of the old Triangle Cafe, this 1950s-style eatery has good food, a wonderfully kitschy interior, and sidewalk seating so you can watch other Route 66 tourists on the highway watching you. Isn't it grand to be here first?

If you're a classic car buff, check out the Dream Machine right next door. A mini-tour of Kingman's more interesting structures has been organized by the historical society, and there's a fine little museum connected to the Kingman Chamber of Commerce. If your itch for history runs a little deeper, pick up a brochure on the old wagon wheel tracks at White Cliffs.

Departing Kingman, continue on the old route through a deep cut to the **McConnico** undercrossing. At the stop, turn west under the interstate and follow Oatman Road— the last and best part of the western Arizona section of old Route 66.

Be forewarned, however. If you are a longtime flatlander

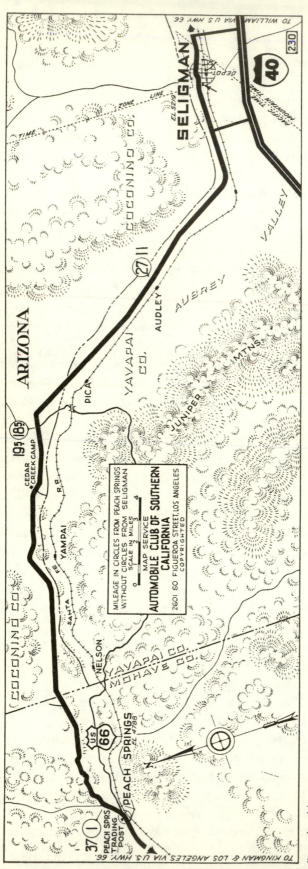

Reproduced by permission

or are driving an RV that handles about like the *Graf Zeppelin* in a high wind, you may want to take the interstate and continue your tour of old Route 66 in Needles. Otherwise, precautions noted, carry on.

If a major part of your driving time until now has been up on the superslab, you'll be surprised how quickly civilization fades once you are away from town. There are real beginnings and endings here on old Route 66, and a truer sense of being alone, dependent on your vehicle and the road itself to take you safely through. Along this stretch especially, there's often the very first glimmer of how it must have been for travelers forty or fifty years ago. As you roll deeper into the desert, a more primitive part of the brain begins to stir. You may find yourself listening more carefully to the engine, checking the gauges, feeling with your hands what's happening on the road just below. By the time you reach **Cool Springs Camp** (which is none of those, but only a trashed ruin now) you may even have heard some mechanical notes never audible to you before. Funny how perfectly good engines can sound rough way out here.

Up to this point, where the grade begins in earnest, your main concern will be the odd jackrabbit or roadrunner grown unused to traffic. But you can soon expect other road companions. Wild burros, brought here by prospectors long ago and turned loose, now number in the thousands. They also blend so well into the desert scrub that it is difficult to see them before they saunter onto the road to inspect you. Protected by the Wild Horse Act, they are not timid. And if you pull over for a moment to take in the view, you may hear them calling to one another—announcing your arrival perhaps. For they are born tourist hustlers with an acquired taste for the junk food we are known always to have with us.

This segment of old Route 66 is also just the ticket for drivers or riders with an affinity for switchbacks. And if you fancy yourself something of a canyon buster, the run over Sitgreaves Pass into Oatman may be just what you've been waiting for. Especially if you've dreamed of the twisties on the famous Stelvio Road in the Alps, but cannot yet make the fare to Europe.

All right, then, just imagine an alpine road dropped

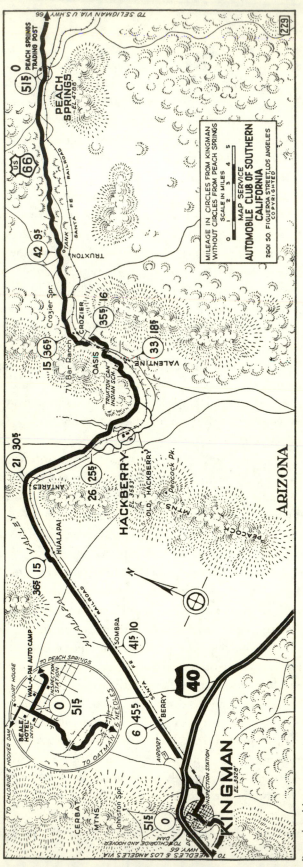

Reproduced by permission

down into the middle of the American desert. Instead of black ice and maniacal Italian bus drivers, here you'll be dealing with scattered patches of shoulder gravel, rock-hounds in 4 × 4s, and the occasional band of wide-angle choppers. Still, it's often said that the highway surface, curves, and gradients are a miniature version of the Stelvio run.

In the old days, when cars and trucks had little power, even in first gear, the only way up the 3,500-foot grade from Oatman east was in reverse—a craft mastered so well by locals that they could do it at top speed, by rearview mirror only, while dangling one arm loosely out the window. So, as you drive these marvelous old switch-backs, imagine how city-bred easterners must have felt when they veered into a blind, cliff-hanging curve, only to encounter some mad local coming full steam up the mountain *backward*. Commercial laundries at the bottom of the hill must have done a hell of a business.

Switchbacks still ahead for the moment, continue on to **Ed's Camp** (which is both), a few miles short of Sitgreaves Pass. As you'll quickly notice, Ed's is more than a way station for the overheated and overfed travler. It's also a desert-style flea market with all sorts of collectible debris lying in wait for those with a skosh more room in the back.

Just over the summit, you'll also discover the earthly remains of **Goldroad.** Just a few adobe walls and stone foundations are here now, the owners having decided to save on their taxes by burning the town to the ground. So much for architectural and cultural heritage.

Once at the center of rich finds, this entire area had already been fairly well picked over by prospectors when one José Jerez discovered a major new outcropping. The town boomed again as everyone cashed in on the find. Everyone but José, that is, who spent his small share and then walked out by the road one night, sat down, and chugalugged a bottle of rat poison. *C'est la prospérité.*

Down in **Oatman** the main street is a curious jam-up of gun-toting locals and camera-ridden tourists. Plus, of course, the omnipresent burros who, while happily hus-tling everybody, should be fed *carrots* only. Take a while to explore the character of this place that, booming or broke, has always gone its own way. Check out the Gold

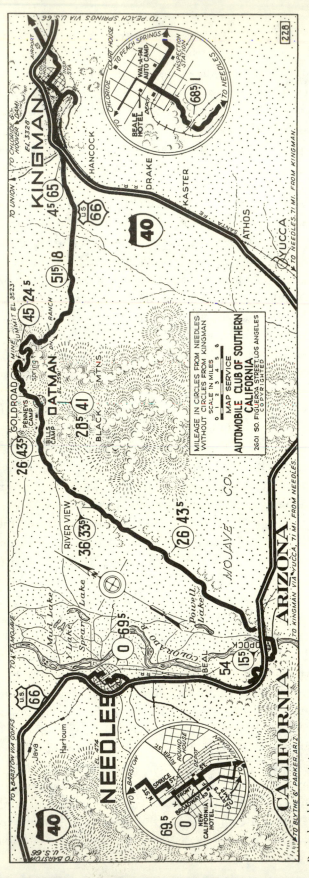

Strike for interesting art or try your luck at the western shooting gallery. And be sure to look in on the Oatman Hotel, best known as the honeymoon hideaway of Clark Gable and Carole Lombard. Town talent also puts on a floozie revue, alternating with staged gunfights, usually on weekends.

Heading west out of town, turn south at the Y toward **Topock,** where you'll rejoin I-40 westbound into California. Except for the pavement, this sobering desert section of old Route 66 has not changed since Dust Bowl days. If it's anytime around summer, you'll know why the Joads walked out into the Colorado River shallows and just stood there after driving this stretch. The road from Oatman to Topock can be as tough as any road ever gets.

And at night, from the early 1930s until the mid-1950s, this desolate section of road had everybody reaching for their car radios. Back in AM-radio days, you might have some trouble with static if a thunderstorm rolled in over the route. Otherwise, a broadcast signal wasn't limited to ninety miles or so, as FM is. Instead, AM reached out hundreds or—with a good skip—even thousands of miles to eager listeners.

So as you rolled along the highway, network shows like *Jack Benny* and *Sam Spade, Private Eye* and *Duffy's Tavern* could be tuned in virtually anywhere along old Route 66, even here in this godforsaken desert. And you didn't worry so much about getting lost out here if *Amos 'N Andy* were along with you.

Radio rode with you, shortening the miles and bringing something both extraordinary and familiar to the solitude of a two-lane road.

8

CALIFORNIA

Crossing into California isn't the adventure it once was. But neither is it the terror.

Back in the Dust Bowl days there were barricades out on the road. Armed men, too—local recruits mostly—many hired from the worst of the saloons along the highway. Men itching to call out anyone they didn't know, shoot anything that moved, club anyone who might resist. California was terrified, all right. Frightened silly that this stirred-up cloud of people would discover that it could be an army. An army that could take the whole state if it wanted. And right here, close to the border, is where that fear showed most.

A man with a Sam Browne belt and heavy, rib-kicking boots would be looking down the long, ragged line of overloaded, steaming jalopies. Peering into the first car. Studying some patient, fumbling man at the wheel, the enduring but crumpled face of his wife, and the sit-still-now looks of the children, their eyes shifting from the glinting badge to the black billy club now in momentary repose at the open side window.

You folks planning to cross? Stupid question. What would they be doing in line for near a day, if they didn't intend to cross? But barricades and shotguns are the tools of men who are themselves desperate in some way. Intelligence is rarely deputized.

You folks got any money? Uh-huh. How much? Let me see it.

The money is produced. There isn't a lot, even by Okie standards, but it's something. A little change, a few sweat-soaked bills folded into a waistband pocket still stretched from the watch it no longer holds. The driver sneaks a quick glance back over his shoulder at the family in the next car down the line, fearing that he is somehow holding them up.

Looking more carefully at the kids now. Any sign of disease? Any excuse at all to turn the car back, send these people off to some other border? But there is no reason. Thinking of his own family, perhaps, the man with the badge steps back and without expression waves the car on.

But before he is out of second gear, the freed driver can see in his mirror that the car behind has already been turned away and out of line. Sent back to Arizona or somewhere else. Sent to anywhere-but-here. For some reason. For any reason . . .

Everything has changed since then, of course. Or it has seemed to. The agricultural inspection station was even moved some years back. Crossing into California is no longer a problem, unless you happen to be an inveterate apple-snacker or cactus-collector. And, thanks to equal opportunity, some of the agricultural inspectors are more than pleasant; they are lovely. A nice touch. A bit of tinseltown, way out here on the desert.

Few travelers think of the desert as being the *real* California, though. Not the California of laid-back surfers, iron-kneed skateboarders, and delectable beach bunnies. That California still lies well to the west. The desert here is a harsh, tough place. A place where the well-watered California dream has not yet made its mark. The other California is closer to the sea, where life is easier, where both cars and humans seem to endure forever.

At a traditional picnic held in Los Angeles by emigrants from Iowa, some have been heard to say that California is a crazy place. Perhaps that's so. Perhaps all those people from Iowa are being held captive out here, without anyone's knowledge. Perhaps, as someone also suggested, the continent has tilted so that everything not screwed tightly down comes sliding right into Southern California. If that's true, it has produced a wondrous blend.

So welcome to California. Spiritual home of the Sing-Along *Messiah*. Birth state of right-turn-on-red.

It's an interesting place.

NEEDLES TO
SAN BERNARDINO

Some regular desert travelers believe **Needles** was named for the prickly desert heat. Not true, though. The town was named for the spiky mountains to the south, beyond the graceful, silver-arched bridge over the Colorado River. That same bridge, by the way, once carried old Route 66 and still serves as a pipeline support. Notice also that from Needles west, there are over a hundred miles of open desert with few services before Barstow, so you may want to see to your vehicle's fluids and your own before heading out.

For the city portion of old Route 66 through Needles, take the third exit (US 95) northbound after crossing the river and continue through town on Broadway. Watch for the 66 and Palm motels and the once-magnificent El Garces, formerly a Fred Harvey hotel, now only an append-age of the Amtrak station. For breakfast, the Hungry Bear Restaurant, next to the Travelodge near the west end of town, specializes in homemade biscuits and gravy and is frequented by many locals.

Beyond Needles, return to I-40 and exit at US 95 for a forty-mile segment of the old route that ran through **Goffs** until 1931. An interesting, crusty desert town, Goffs is a survivor in its own right—one of those places that wouldn't know how to give up. Once, because it is usually at least fifteen degrees cooler than Needles, Goffs was a regular little summer resort. Now, even with double bypass surgery and air conditioning everywhere on the desert, the town carries on somehow.

To continue on the old route, cross under I-40 near **Fenner.** You'll be on a well-known section posted as National Old Trails, of which this highway was a part before becoming Route 66. Rolling on toward **Essex,** though, keep a lookout ahead. Just a few miles beyond the interstate exit, where the road curves down and away

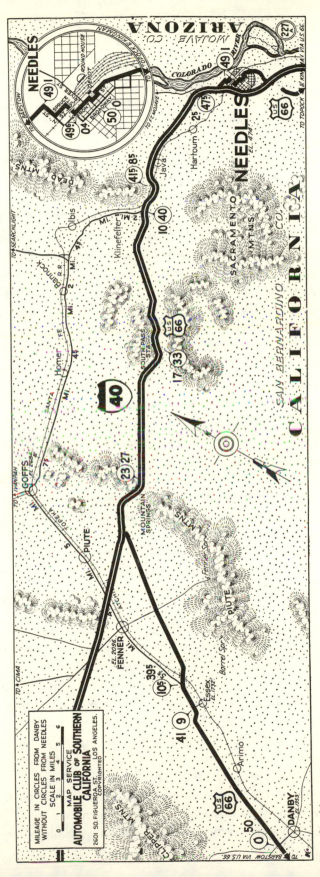

to the right, you'll get a first look at what lay in wait for the pioneer or the Dust Bowl family. Imagine the feeling: just when you have struggled past the terrible grade west of Needles and believe the worst to be over, you see what must yet be endured.

Out beyond the shimmering, glass-hard desert floor in front of you is another range of mountains, a thousand feet higher than those you just crossed. And beyond them yet another great barrier range, higher still. Peaks to 10,000 feet, some still carrying the snows of winter. Perhaps you tremble a little at the thought of what it will be like to go on. Most did tremble. And some, taking in the seeming endlessness of these trials, just stopped their creaking wagons or steaming old cars and without a word to anyone, walked away into the desert and disappeared. It was not a good end. But it was a way to have it over with, and that's all some could find for themselves in this merciless place. Just an end to it all.

On toward **Chambless,** though, the desert takes on a different meaning. Nearly fifty years ago, the desert here meant not death but a chance at life. It was during World War II and a very bad time for America, just then. General Erwin Rommel, Hitler's Desert Fox, was loose with his Panzer Corps, racing almost unopposed across North Africa toward the unlimited supply of oil needed by the Nazi war machine. If we could not support the beleaguered British there soon, the war would most certainly be lost.

Enter the singular General George S. Patton, "Old Blood-and-Guts" himself. Patton had been reared in this part of California and knew that the Mojave was not only similar to North Africa, it could be worse. So he pressed every tank, truck, motorcycle, and reconnaissance aircraft he could find into service as part of his Desert Training Center. Over two million men were trained to survive in the 10,000 square miles of desert surrounding you now. In the end, the Great Mojave did its job. And Patton and the Second Corps did theirs, sweeping through North Africa as if they knew their way around—with no surprises their own desert hadn't already shown them.

Now the Mojave is quiet again, a place for reflection. In **Amboy,** you may even reflect on buying the town, if it's still for sale. While you're considering an offer, stop

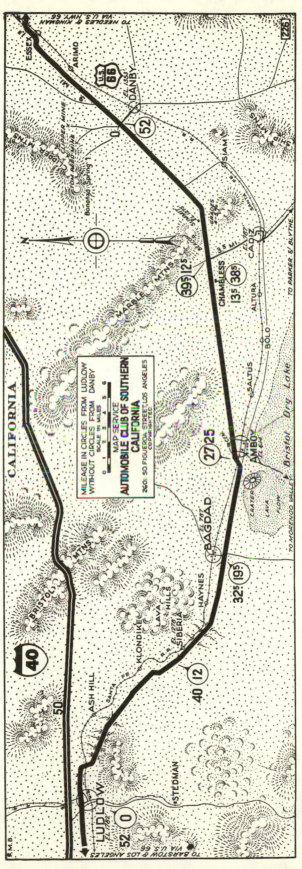

Reproduced by permission

in at Roy's Cafe. It's the best place in town for eats and stories.

Halfway from Amboy to **Siberia** lie the overgrown remains of Bagdad, inspiration for the film *Bagdad Café*, which you may want to see on videocassette. Actually shot in Newberry Springs, the film is a marvelous tale of human relationships and what kind of endurance and personal responsibility it takes to transform misgivings and self-pity into trust and love. As they do in real life, the road and the desert strip away all but the essentials. Old Route 66 offers a way in and a way out. Everyone is free to choose either direction, with the desert burning away everything else. You may enjoy the movie or, funny as it is, you may find it distressing. Either way, you'll not soon forget it— or this stretch of highway.

A break in the old road occurs at **Ludlow.** To continue on Route 66, cross under I-40, head west over a newer service road, and then cross over the interstate and rejoin the old highway at **Lavic** for a short run to **Newberry Springs.** Recross to the north side of I-40 there, and continue on through **Minneola** and **Coolwater.**

Daggett, now an aging bridesmaid among railroad towns, was once a major transshipment point for the borax trade (Remember reruns of Ronald Reagan hosting *Death Valley Days?*) from Calico to the north. Fat and sassy, Daggett developers learned that the Santa Fe Railway planned a major switching complex there. But the developers drove the price of land so high that the complex was built over at Waterman Junction instead. Later, the new site was given the middle name of the railroad's president, William Barstow Strong. Downtown Daggett now has little more than a homey general store and the Stone Hotel, once a favorite hangout for Death Valley Scotty, Tom Mix, and Wallace Beery.

Just west of Daggett, old Route 66 passes through a Marine Corps depot, so it's best to rejoin the interstate into Barstow, exiting at Main Street. I-40 ends here, with I-15 continuing on to San Bernardino.

For an overnight in **Barstow,** there's El Rancho Motel and Route 66 Visitor Center. Originally built entirely of railroad ties and on the highway at 112 East Main since 1947, the motel and its 100-foot neon sign have been restored and are worth a stop.

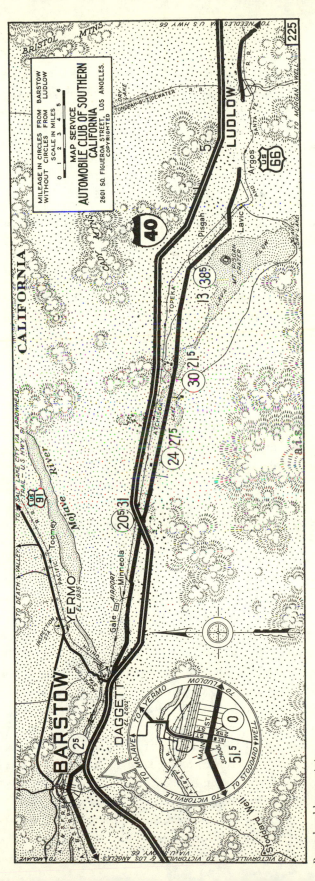

MILEAGE IN CIRCLES FROM BARSTOW
WITHOUT CIRCLES FROM LUDLOW

SCALE IN MILES
0 1 2 3 4 5 6

MAP SERVICE
AUTOMOBILE CLUB OF SOUTHERN
CALIFORNIA
2601 SO. FIGUEROA STREET, LOS ANGELES.
COPYRIGHTED

225

Route 66 continues on Main Street in town, leading west through **Lenwood, Hodge, Helendale,** and **Oro Grande.** It's an easy drive of thirty-eight miles or so on a well-maintained highway. Scenery is mixed: some high desert, some river basin. There'll be plenty of time to speculate on businesses like Honolulu Jim's that once populated this part of the route so long ago. How did the owner happen upon the name? Had he been a sailor stationed at Pearl Harbor? Or, like others in the tourist business along old Route 66, was he simply a master marketer? Ah, Honolulu Jim's. How does it manage to sound so wholesome, yet still carry a slight tinge of something just a bit illicit? Who could resist stopping for a cold ice cream soda, a chocolate malt, and perhaps a lei?

The old route crosses under I-15 to enter **Victorville,** where Main Street to Seventh Street was the alignment through town. Dyed-in-the-wool tourists and borderline necrophiles will surely want to visit Trigger, the stuffed horse—undoubtedly Roy Roger's vision of equine immortality. Otherwise, you may want to keep on going.

If you need some fuel at **Cajon Summit**—even if you don't—take the Oak Hill exit for the old Summit Inn on Mariposa Road since 1952. This was a regular stop when topping the Cajon Pass was still a big deal. Try the cinnamon rolls with coffee. Look at the old road, lean back, imagine how it was.

From Victorville to San Bernardino (San Berdoo to locals), nearly all the old route lies directly beneath I-15. All, that is, except for a five-mile section that has a wonderful feeling of time suspended. Used by locals, this brief stretch turns up on the east side at the exit just beyond SR 138 at **Cajon Junction.** Twisting along below the newer highway, this old remnant follows the river wash and the Santa Fe tracks southeast to Cajon Mountain where you must rejoin I-15. If you've not had time for the longer loops through Goffs or Amboy or Helendale, be sure to take a few minutes for this brief interlude. If anyone ever films *Twilight Zone Meets Son of Route 66,* this piece of road is where it will be shot.

At the **Devore** exit, you may follow old Route 66 again along Cajon Boulevard and southbound Mt. Vernon Avenue, but there is little sense of the old road remaining.

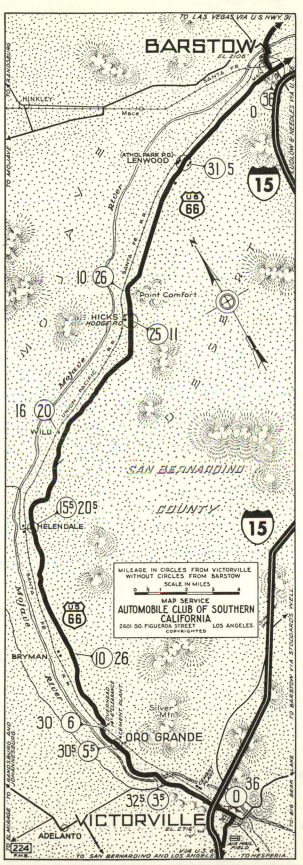

A more convenient route is to exit at 5th Street, which flows into Foothill Boulevard (SR 66) and the old route.

SAN BERNARDINO TO SANTA MONICA

A city in cultural transition, **San Bernardino** has often found itself trapped between two opposing mentalities. On one side is the kind of thinking that led city officials to burn down a landmark Route 66 motel on Mt. Vernon Avenue—just so the fire department could have some practice on a slow day. On the other side (most fortunately) is a civic heritage movement, which among other projects, guided the restoration of the famous California Theater. Located at 562 West 4th Street, adjacent to the old route, the California was designed by John Paxton Perrine and completed in 1928.

In those days, movie palaces commonly employed vaudeville acts to draw a larger audience, and the California was a major break-in theater for new talent. When sneak previews became common in the 1930s, the Santa Fe Railway became a virtual commuter line for all the stars who trekked out from Hollywood to San Bernardino to find glory or disaster in the first public showing of their latest films.

Will Rogers's last public appearance was at the California in 1935. Will headlined a star-filled benefit performance, featuring everyone from Buster Crabbe and Jane Withers, to unknowns like Rita Cansino, who would be later recognized as Rita Hayworth. Less than two months later Will was gone, killed in a plane crash on Alaska's North Slope with his pilot and good friend, Wiley Post. But the theater is still here, fully restored (now air conditioned, too) and rich with the original voice of its great Wurlitzer pipe organ. And thanks to local support, there's usually a good show on stage. So, if you're a little jaded from driving the desert, plan to spend the night here and take in a live performance. Most shows are not expensive, and it's a grand place to breathe in a moment from Southern California's golden past.

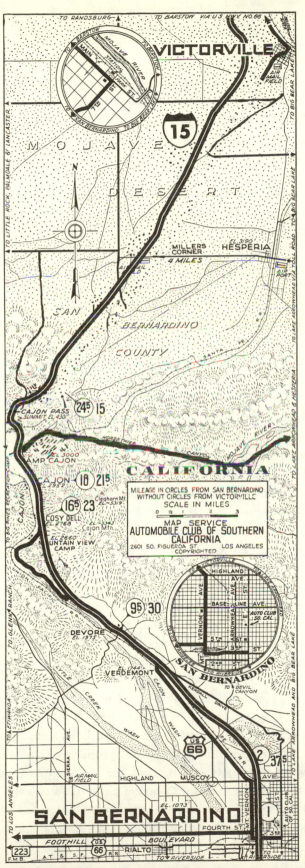

Crossing L.A. on eighty miles of city streets can take more than a full day, and is no longer so safe as it was when the first edition of the *Route 66 Traveler's Guide* was published. And there can be frustrating jam-ups between seven and ten in the morning and from three to seven on weekday afternoons. Mondays aren't so bad, but Murphy's Law rules supreme on Fridays.

If you are eager to complete your journey and simply want to get to the sea breezes at the end of the route in Santa Monica, take I-10 from San Bernardino all the way. Once in Santa Monica, exit on northbound Lincoln Boulevard, turn west again on Colorado, and continue to Ocean Avenue. Once there, consult the last few pages of this guide to choose the best way to end your journey. It's an easy route on the freeways and you can be there in a couple of hours.

With a half day or more, there is a nice combination route to follow that will keep you on the old alignment most of the way with least difficulty. From San Bernardino, continue west along Foothill Boulevard (SR 66). Just east of Pepper Avenue is the site of the twin to Holbrook's Wigwam Village.

Although settlement of this region in Southern California stems directly from cultivation of the first orange groves and vineyards in the state, nearly all of that milk-and-honey life is gone now—replaced by a drive toward security rather than quality of life as the prime consideration. Huge, lighted signs on outsized buildings along this stretch carry martial nouns like SENTINEL, FORTRESS, and GUARDIAN, which appear with the same frequency as the word *Acme* once did in Warner Bros. cartoons. Now and then a light, earthy noun like SPRINGTIME pops up. But not often.

If you recall the running Jack Benny gag about a train that went through "An-a-heim, Azu-za, and Coook-a-monga," you're in luck. **Rancho Cucamonga** is next along the route. This section of Foothill Boulevard was originally a Mormon farm-to-market road, hacked out of dense brush by settlers in 1852. Later, much of the area was given over to vineyards. Look for the Virginia Dare Winery at Haven Avenue, it's one of California's oldest.

At Archibald Avenue, there's a Richfield Oil station built in the 1920s. And the Sycamore Inn—a very special

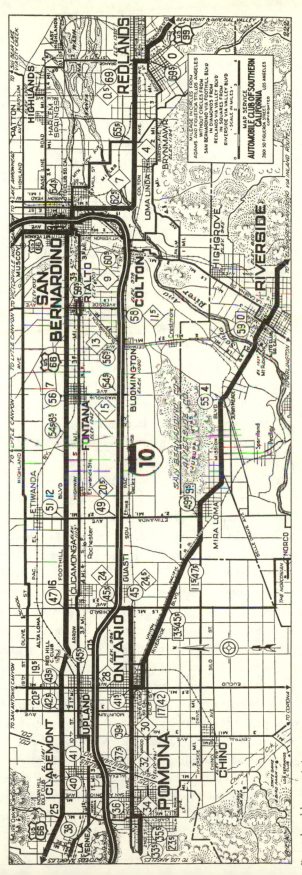

place and once a San Bernardino Stage stop—has been offering good food and friendly service for over 140 years. If it's getting close on to suppertime, be sure to make a stop. Just as interesting and inviting in its own curio style is the Magic Lamp—catty-corner across the street.

In **Upland,** at Euclid Avenue, a statue of Madonna of the Trail (no relation to the star-crossed singer) marks the end of National Old Trails and stands as a tribute to the pioneer women of the westering movement. Also, if you are any kind of aviation buff, one of the finest collections in the West of vintage aircraft is displayed at the Planes of Fame Museum (best call for hours) adjoining the airport in **Chino,** about four miles south on Euclid. This field is home to a number of internationally known airshow/racing pilots and collectors, so there can be interesting traffic in the landing pattern on most any day.

Approaching **Glendora,** you'll have a choice of routes. For the older and more interesting 1930s alignment, turn north on Amelia Avenue and then west again on a somewhat displaced Foothill Boulevard. Some of these main-street buildings haven't changed in a hundred years, which is what the good people of Glendora intended. Jog south again on Citrus Avenue to join the newer Alosta Avenue alignment, and continue west.

In **Monrovia,** jog north on Shamrock Avenue, then west again on Foothill Boulevard. Just beyond Myrtle Avenue, at 311 W. Foothill, you'll find the justly famous Aztec Hotel, designed by Robert Stacy-Judd in 1926 as an all-out tourist grabber for the new Route 66. It's now on the National Register and worth a stop whether you are on surface streets or taking the interstate. The patio is delightful and you'll half-expect to find Sydney Greenstreet resident in the Elephant Bar and Restaurant.

Jog south as Foothill enters **Pasadena,** and continue west. You're now on the Rose Parade route, so you might not want to try this on New Year's Day—unless New Year's happens to fall on a Sunday. Why? Because this is also genteel Pasadena where, in an age-old deal with local churches, the Tournament of Roses committee agreed never to do it on Sunday. Why? Too immoral? No, parishioners were concerned that the parade might have frightened the horses tied up during services. Parade or no, take time for architectural and museum tours here if at all possible. Much can be found that is truly extraordinary.

Near Fair Oaks Avenue, the alignments of old Route 66 divide. An early version turned south on Fair Oaks, following Huntington Drive and North Broadway into downtown **Los Angeles**—past once-famous Ptomaine Tommy's restaurant, where the Chili Size was invented back during the Great Depression. Another routing continued west on Colorado Boulevard to Eagle Rock, where it turned south toward the Central L.A. district.

Tommy's is gone now, and if driving time is short, take the 1941 Arroyo Seco Parkway (SR 11) south to the Pasadena Freeway, transitioning to the westbound Hollywood Freeway and the Santa Monica Boulevard exit. But there's also a neat combined route. Just take Fair Oaks south to Mission Street. There, the Fair Oaks Pharmacy is a step back in time and space. In addition to irresistible soda-fountain treats, you'll find a turn-of-the-century interior brought here intact from Joplin, Missouri. Several good restaurants are nearby, as well. When you're ready, take Mission west and continue on the Pasadena/Hollywood Freeways.

To follow an interesting 1930s alignment, however, take the exit leading to westbound Sunset Boulevard. Looming just a block south at Glendale Boulevard is the famous Angelus Temple built by Aimee Semple McPherson. Probably no one soared to quite the evangelistic heights reached by Sister Aimee, whose charisma and career survived publicized divorces, a self-described kidnapping of epic proportions, and dozens of simultaneous lawsuits. By 1941, the temple itself had become a prime tourist attraction along old Route 66.

Continue on Sunset and turn west on Santa Monica Boulevard. Above you, along here, is the famous HOLLYWOOD sign. Imported as a name from a Chicago suburb, the name was originally Hollywoodland, a real estate development west of Griffith Park. A landmark for motorists, pilots, and the starry-eyed, the sign has stood through thick and thin. With maintenance first discontinued in 1939, the sign has survived vandals, petty bureaucrats, destructive Santa Ana winds, and the stigma added by an actress's high dive from the top of the first letter to her

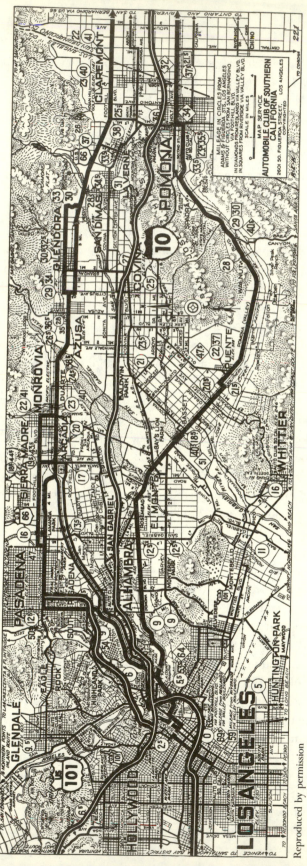

Reproduced by permission

death below. Now, with the LAND portion gone, the sign has been repaired and remains a beacon for a city that has officially never existed.

Continue west on Santa Monica Boulevard, through the boutique and little-theater district, past shops always on the trailing edge of trendy.

Near the western boundary of **Beverly Hills,** seven blocks beyond Beverly Drive on Walden, is an architectural treat for fans of the siltent-movie period. It's the Spadena house, a delightful Hansel and Gretel cottage designed by Henry Oliver in 1921. Originally, it was the office of Irvin C. Willat Productions in Culver City, before being moved to its present site on the southeast corner of Carmelita. In late afternoon light, you can practically smell the ginger-bread baking.

Farther along is glistening **Century City,** constructed by Alcoa in a flukish deal on the Twentieth Century–Fox backlot. Since a new Mercedes is common carriage here, the area is known chiefly for its upscale work eithic— you are even less what you drive than where you park— and for Harry's Bar and American Grill across from the Century Plaza Hotel.

Harry's is very dark and very good. It's also where they hold a well-known annual contest to see who can write most like Ernest Hemingway. . . . *In the hazy, brown light of afternoon we would go to Harry's to do the watching and the writing. Tight-breasted waitresses would smile at us as they walked by. They had the long legs and full calves of dancers, which was their true profession, and we always smiled back. After a while, we would forget about the writing and just do the watching. . . .* Some say the contest affects everybody.

After you're done with whatever you decide to do at Harry's, though, continue on through West Los Angeles on the old route toward **Santa Monica.**

There is a natural tendency to want old Route 66 to extend from shore to shore. But it didn't truly begin at Lake Michigan and never ended at the Pacific Ocean. What we've learned since the first edition of the *Traveler's Guide* is that the highway did not terminate on Santa Monica Boulevard at Ocean Avenue as an old photograph had indicated. The picture, as it happens, was a fake. After being extended from Los Angeles to Santa Monica in 1935,

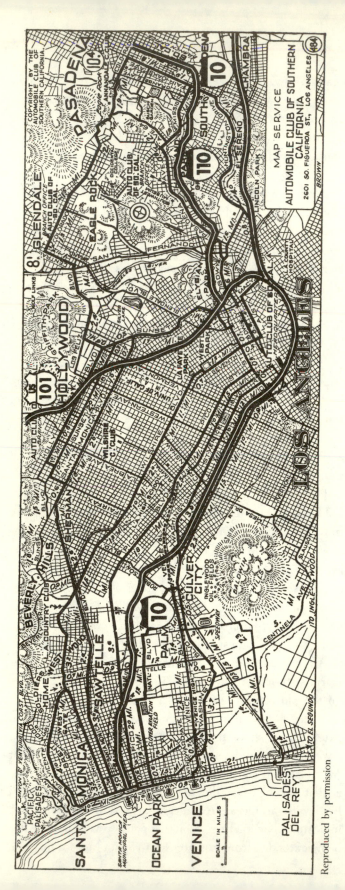

Route 66 joined US 101A on Lincoln Boulevard south-bound, ending at Olympic Boulevard. Sadly, that intersection and its 1950s coffee shop are now fairly well trashed by the freeway. But Route 66 has always been a highway of fantasy. So you are free, especially here in movieland, to choose your own ending to this adventure.

A block north and straight west a few blocks on Colorado is the Santa Monica Pier. If you're a Redford and Newman fan, you'll want to take a ride on the beautifully restored carousel—it's the one used in George Roy Hill's 1973 film *The Sting*. The pier itself is a Southern California tradition and full of curiosities. It's also as far west as you can go without getting wet.

To the north, across Ocean Avenue at the end of Santa Monica Boulevard, is a plaque memorializing Route 66 as Will Rogers Highway. Actually, the plaque was part of a promotion for the 1952 film *The Story of Will Rogers*. If you're observant, you may even have noticed a highway marker announcing such in John Ford's production of *The Grapes of Wrath*, released in 1940. So if the feeling of Route 66 in its early years appeals most to you, end your journey along the path in Palisades Park just beyond the plaque, above the Pacific.

Before leaving this area, however, be sure to make a pilgrimage to Will Rogers's ranch, now preserved with the cooperation of the Rogers family as a California state park. Drive northwest on Ocean Avenue three blocks and, at California Avenue, turn left and head down the hill to Pacific Coast Highway. Continue on PCH a little over three miles, turn right onto Sunset Boulevard (yes, it's the same one), and wind inland to number 14253, on the left. Signs will guide you up to the ranch itself. Or, most anyone you meet on horseback will gladly direct you.

There's more of a feeling of Will himself—what he loved and what enriched the caring he felt for all of us—here on this lovely 185-acre spread than you'll find anywhere else. Will's little office, where he did most of his writing, is just upstairs. In the early morning, with a light coastal fog hanging in the eucalyptus trees, you can practically feel the words coming through the window and down into this old typewriter.

Wiley Post used to sideslip his new monoplane in from

the southeast, over the polo field, to land deftly on the wide, sloping lawn next to the house. Bring a lunch—you can picnic right on Wiley's runway. The whole place is truly inspiring, and you'll enjoy just wandering about on your own. In spring, when all the flowers bordering the old, board-and-batten ranch house are in bloom, it's a reminder that paradise is not somewhere up, up, and away. It's right here, all around. Some places just help us see it a little more clearly. Will Roger's ranch is one of them.

Before going off to do any sightseeing, though, take time to stroll along the boardwalk or the bluffs in Santa Monica. We'll be parting company here after a grand tour, and it's a way of completing your journey over old Route 66 in a personal way. Watch the people. Take in a sunset. Breathe some fresh air before the city gets hold of it.

Like most travelers who come to Southern California, you may not have exactly arrived. But the sea, the people, and this place all let you know that you are here.

You are definitely here.

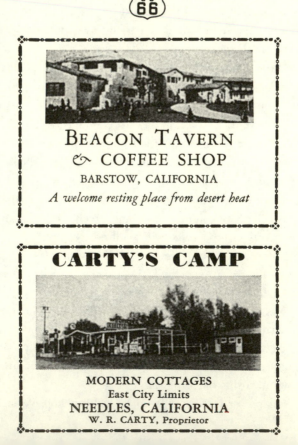

ROADSIDE
COMPANION

ILLINOIS

Highway-building has always been high on any list of priorities for Illinois. But the push for better roads sometimes came less from auto clubs and engineers than from Gangland, USA. With Prohibition in full swing, the likes of Hymie Weiss, Bugs Moran, and Al Capone needed high-speed roadways from Chicago south.

Illegal booze was being collected from neighborhood stills, hijacked from government warehouses, or brought in by speedboat from Canada. And like a bathtub drain, the booze was backing up. The Capone gang, in particular, needed to get their supplies moving.

The power of the gangs during the 1920s was enormous, reaching into every part of society. Today, when drug-running is diffused like an underground cottage industry, the concentration of that power is incomprehensible. But at the height of Capone's career there was no public office, from Chicago's City Hall to the capital at Springfield, that he didn't control or influence.

At the time, Capone was paying $30 million a year—in pretax, preinflation dollars—to the police alone. So if Big Al wanted a fine, new highway to St. Louis for his trucks and armed caravans, there sure as hell was going to be one. And why not make it a bright new US highway as well?

Route US 66 filled the bill, and not surprisingly, the necessary appropriations sailed through the Illinois legislature in record time. Concrete was going down almost before the ink was dry and the rum-runners' convoys were soon rolling to mob distribution centers in St. Louis.

In downstate Illinois, ballrooms, barrooms, and bawdy houses all came under the control of Capone and his confederates. One of the most profitable was the Riviera (a.k.a. the Hideaway) near Gardner on Route 66, and Capone is said to have kept a place on the Kankakee River at Wilmington for his wilder parties—featuring whatever you can imagine, and probably more. If something was illegal, you could bet the crime lord bought it, sold it, or used it.

Capone also had an unusual liking for pastel suits with matching ties, and surrounded himself with equally colorful bodyguards. So when the boys climbed into their speedy Jewetts to accompany Big Al's armor-plated Cadillac on the new Route 66, it looked like rainbow sherbet rolling into town. Still, it was all a deadly business.

The first car was fitted with a cast-iron bumper meant to ram any misguided police flivver, while Capone's Caddy was safely tucked in the middle. The final car bristled with Tommy-gun men as a rear guard—all dressed in shades of yellow, mauve, sea-green, and peach. Not that anyone laughed.

A frequent stop along Route 66 for Capone's entourage was one of the Rossi family businesses around Braidwood. As it happened, the eldest Rossi operated a saloon and grocery store, in addition to several dance halls in which the gang was interested. But what was most intriguing to the mobsters was the way in which Rossi kept his workers in line. Theft and double-dealing in the ranks was always a problem for Capone and the other bosses, so they were impressed by innovative thinking. After all, good gangies were too useful to shoot because of minor infractions.

One story the mobsters were sure to have heard concerned the loss of bottles from a private stock of homemade wine that the senior Rossi kept handy for "medicinal purposes." After weeks of trying to discover the culprit, he simply laced a few bottles with a powerful Italian laxative and waited. The next day, when one of his drivers couldn't stay out of the bathroom for more than a few minutes, Rossi pitched the thief out on his ear.

The mob certainly could have used that kind of talent. But even though the Rossis' dance halls mysteriously burned a short time later, the gang was never able to recruit any of the family and had to be content, as we are, with the story.

Farther south on Route 66, however, the gang gave the folks at Funks Grove an uneasy time. In the maple-syrup business since 1891, the Funk family is still known nationwide for the quality of their "sirup," and the entire supply normally sells out before summer each year.

Now life in the sugarbush is a pastoral one and no one in Funks Grove had ever come in contact with the mob. The Funks only knew, as did everyone else in Illinois, that mere mention of Capone's movements could bring immediate death, or worse. Fortunately, the mobsters usually rolled at night and on the sly.

What the Funks didn't know was that, in addition to colorful garments, Scarface Capone also had a whopper of a sweet tooth. It would have explained the slow file of heavy automobiles the Funks saw winding ponderously up the drive toward their saphouse.

Once stopped, pastels appeared everywhere and a gunsel from the lead car ordered several cases of super-sweet maple syrup. The purchase made and loaded, a large man in yellow suit and matching fedora signaled with his cigar from the middle car, and the cortege wound slowly back out to the highway to head north.

The elder Funks looked at one another and decided on the spot that there was no one in any of the cars that they could ever recognize. In fact, maybe the line of cars hadn't been there at all . . .

A good decision for syrup lovers everywhere.

After Capone was sent to prison and the Great Depression began, his empire quickly came apart. Benedict's

Standard Station in McLean noticed a drop in the quality of hoodlums stopping for gas. The molls, with their bee-sting lips and plucked eyebrows, looked shabbier in cloth coats instead of furs, and the men often wore unpressed, threadbare suits without ties.

For a time they tried valiantly to shake down the station owner. But the eldest Benedict, a hickory-tough Kentuckian, would have none of it. He had no use for freelancers especially, since they were often less pre-dictable, more dangerous. So he met them at the door with a double-barreled 12-gauge. The station was vandal-ized now and again but the gunsels soon gave up.

From then on, the Benedicts recall that the class of travelers along Route 66 through downstate Illinois took a turn for the better. Glenn Miller passed through, always the gentleman. So did Cole Porter, in a very stylish linen suit, driving a Jaguar 140 with professional aplomb. Elvis stopped by in later years, looking boyish and a little dis-connected.

Shortly after that, sections of the new interstate high-way began opening. The small towns of downstate Illinois were no longer in the mainstream. And all too soon, Route 66 began to disappear.

Few places along old Route 66 offer so grand an entrance for the traveler as St. Louis. It's like approaching a citadel, with the Mississippi River as a moat—and the Chain of Rocks Bridge to cross over. Even the city's water-intake towers, just south of the bridge, are built in the style of medieval castles.

Chain of Rocks Bridge was completed in 1929, just in time for the Great Depression, amid rumors, legends, and myths that persist to this day. Recent tragedies have only added to the stories. Flowers mysteriously appeared on the anniversary of a workman's death in a fall from the main span. Military aircraft being ferried to the East Coast for tests got stuck at the bend. And the bend itself is fascinating. Few bridges change course in midstream. Yet Chain of Rocks does. Why?

Some of the myths, now put to rest, suggest that the twenty-four-degree bend was an afterthought, or the result of a threat to the closest water-intake tower, or that a squabble over property rights left the bridge no place to land on the Missouri side. Another rumor was that the engineers failed to find sufficient bedrock for their creation.

All untrue. Instead, it appears that the bridge, if constructed in a straight line, would have presented a threat to safe navigation of the river where currents were strong and tricky. So the Army Corps of Engineers recommended the bend; it was incorporated in the original plans and specifications, and you can see for yourself that it worked out all right.

But for promoters, the bridge was not a good investment. Even without the Depression, a toll bridge that offered no direct route through or around St. Louis was doomed. The enterprise went broke and was refinanced with more than a million-dollar loss. Yet the graceful structure and its tree-lined approaches somehow went on to capture the fancy of Route 66 travelers. The Chain of Rocks Bridge remains a favorite. Today, you can even hike-bike the bridge over a new trail.

Southwest of St. Louis, Route 66 runs through Ozark country, among the richest in scenery to be found anywhere. Each spring when the dogwood is in flower, the story goes, St. Peter has to lock heaven's gates to keep Ozark souls from returning home to a greater beauty.

By contrast, some homesteads along this same stretch are also among the poorest to be found anywhere. All of which makes the Great Jumbo Shrimp Disaster an event they still talk about from Rolla to Joplin.

Just east of the Hooker Cut, not far from Devils Elbow, the old highway twists along the edge of a steep ravine. And not long ago, a big tractor-trailer rig loaded with over 40,000 pounds of frozen Gulf shrimp overshot a tight bend.

Slithering and crashing down the steep side of the ravine, the rig finally hit bottom with a bang that brought out just about everyone in the territory. Good thing, too, for the trailer caught fire shortly and it was only by quick action and a half-mile of garden hose that a handful of volunteers managed to put it out.

After a brief survey of the wreck, the locals realized the truck was going to be down there for quite a spell— and they began to think about what it would be like to have tons of burnt, rotting fish for a neighbor. So they began discussing ways to get the mess cleaned up and out of there. It was about then that someone discovered that if you knocked the outer layer of burned shrimp off each block of ice, the rest was still frozen solid.

A light bulb appeared over the head of every mountain man simultaneously. And in less than an hour, the trail up from the wreck looked as though it had been taken over by a colony of ants. Men struggled up the hillside to deposit their treasure boxes in the backs of pickup trucks. As filled trucks pulled away, more came to take their places. A makeshift road was eventually cut to reach the ravaged truck, and after that the loading went even faster.

By morning the battered trailer lay empty. Of course, in the early 1950s, not many of the folks in this region owned freezers, and few had ever tasted shrimp in any form. But the race was on to beat the thawing process.

Soon every family table featured fried shrimp, stewed shrimp, shrimp cocktail, and a kind of shrimpy Waldorf salad. Some, it is said, even tried shrimp pancakes and shrimp fritters. In the end, fishermen were even baiting their trout hooks with the stuff just to finish off the sorry mess.

The shrimp-truck disaster, everything considered, served up a hillbilly feast to beat all.

The devil figures prominently in many stories from the Ozark region and Route 66 is no exception. Devils Elbow has been known for years as a lovely but difficult stretch of the old highway east of Hooker. Unfortunately, Devils Elbow is a term that refers not so much to the highway as to the river below.

Back in the 1800s, when rivermen brought timber and goods down the Big Piney River, they got pretty good at the job. With strings of log rafts nearly a mile long, and a man in back with a stout snub-pole, they could negotiate every bend in the river with ease. Well, they could until the devil tossed a boulder off a cliff and down into the river—right in the middle of the river's sharpest bend.

When the Big Piney was running full, the devil's new obstacle posed no problem; the boatmen rounded the bend slick as could be. But when the waters were down, the blamed rock would tear up a whole string of rafts, ruining any chance of profit, and generally put the fear of God and dark angels back into everyone.

So, if you drive along this section someday, it's best to remember that Route 66 is up on the rib cage somewhere. Devils Elbow is down on the Big Piney where it's always been.

Attention Elvis fans! If you're a true believer and expect the King to show up any day, you may be looking in all the wrong places. Most anyone in these parts will tell you so because, near the peak of his popularity, Elvis played the Shrine Mosque in Springfield. And it's the place to watch.

Probably the best promoted of all the entertainment facilities along old Route 66, the 4,000-seat Mosque evolved from a home for Abou Ben Adhem Temple to a major stop for opera and dance companies, swing bands, and politicians. Just about every imaginable act was booked here at one time or another, from Spike Jones and his City Slickers to Archduke Felix of Austria.

But other than the night that Missouri-born Harry Truman appeared here in 1952, the hottest booking of all time was old swivel-hips himself. Elvis rolled into town aboard a two-story bus, with his entire band, road crew, and personal attendants of every kind. But he was not happy.

Accounts differ here. Some say box-office figures were not as promised; others suggest that there was a kink in some relationship of the moment. But everyone agrees that Elvis was thoroughly annoyed and his performance showed it. With barely a courtesy encore, the King let it be known that he hated, hated, hated Springfield and sure as hell wouldn't play this burg again. Bubba.

Springfielders didn't exactly mourn on their side either. The Elvis caravan rolled out on Route 66 and the matter was largely forgotten—except by one picker in the band who wouldn't let it rest. When a new facility was built in Springfield, he went to work on his boss. For months, the band member soft-soaped Presley. At long last the picker, who'd lived in Springfield and couldn't stand to hear the town taking continued abuse, resorted to pure begging. *Aw, please. You'll love it. Trust me. Just give Springfield another chance.* That sort of thing.

Elvis probably had all of that he could stand; he either

had to let a good sideman go or play Springfield again. The King caved in. A date was scheduled at the new venue and once again Elvis and company hit town. This time everything went swimmingly. Elvis was happy. The band and road crew were happy, and everyone present knew that the night had been a roaring success.

At the close of the performance an almost-tearful Elvis promised—*promised*—that no matter what, he'd come back to Springfield. So this is the place to watch. Because you know, whatever else is said about the King, he always kept his word.

Over near the Kansas border, Carthage is known for its hospitality and magnificent courthouse. It should also be known as a place where love stories begin. In the spring of 1939, a sweet one caught everyone's attention.

The night was dark and stormy, as it rightly should have been, for the devil's legion was certainly abroad. Granville d'Avenue and his shining new bride Melissa were headed west on Route 66, eager to see the real West—especially the wild country around Flagstaff that they'd read about in Zane Grey novels.

The two youngsters had been married only a few hours before by a justice of the peace in St. James, where they'd scampered through early evening showers to share a wedding cupcake, safe from the downpour in their second-hand Studebaker.

Just off Route 66 in Carthage, they began searching for an auto court they could afford. But there wasn't a single vacancy. In sleepy desperation, Gran turned into a street that looked safe and crawled into the backseat of the old Studebaker with Melissa to sleep, or whatever. But brilliant flashes of lightning and jolting thunderclaps made it impossible for them to sleep, or whatever.

Gran looked into the crystal-green eyes of his bride and resolved to find a better place for their very first night together. He noticed a light burning in a fine old Victorian home just across the street and they both hoped the residents could suggest a place for them to stay.

It was not to be. As they stepped from the car, a lightning bolt hurtled down—illuminating Gran and Melissa with an eerie light and instantly dispatching the old

Studebaker to used-car limbo. Miraculously, the two youngsters made it as far as the house with the great round window where they collapsed in sweet unison and their two hearts stopped beating forever.

The tragic story soon made its rounds in Carthage, but talk was not all that the owners had inherited from the storm's dark event. Ghostly sounds were soon heard in the home where Gran and Melissa had sought shelter. And not just ordinary sounds, mind you, but such love-sounds as might be heard if a marriage not consummated in this life were extended into the next.

These ghostly activities continued for nearly a year. Then the sounds changed abruptly as what everyone now believed to be the voices of Gran and Melissa were joined by a third—the unmistakable cry of a newborn child. The course of true love, even among ghosts, cannot be denied.

Later owners of the home reported that the three ghosts seemed happy and that the girlish voice was be-coming more mature. In 1958, the daughter's voice was heard for the last time. Perhaps children conceived even in ghostlock leave home, just as mortal children do. Or perhaps the green-eyed daughter of Gran and Melissa simply wanted to see the West her parents had missed.

Only one thing is certain. The home adopted by Gran d'Avenue and his bride still stands near the crossing of Route 66 and US 71. The restored Queen Anne Victorian is now popular with travelers as a bed-and-breakfast, named for its ethereal tenants—the Grand Avenue Inn.

Americans are quick to throw out anything older than the family dog—and roads are no exception. Once Route 66 was decertified as a US highway, nothing protected it as a national treasure.

One structure consigned to the wrecker's ball was the very last of the rainbow-style bridges built in the Riverton area. A main bridge and another span had already fallen to progress.

Often called Graffiti Bridge, it found use as a kind of concrete bulletin board announcing who might be doing what to whom. During the American Bicentennial, in fact, the whole thing was painted red, white, and blue—probably by local girls who were tired of seeing their names displayed there.

Yet regardless of pleas from the community, the span was scheduled for demolition. Government officials were committed to building a new bridge. The reason given was that the old structure didn't meet federal standards—not that it mattered, since the route was no longer a federal highway anyhow.

In short, someone had decided there would damn well

be a new bridge and that was that. The old one would have to come down.

Undaunted, the Kansas Historical Route 66 Association went on searching for a way to stop the destruction, and in the federal regulations, found a way to do it. Right there in official black and white, the regulations stated that when a new span is to be constructed, the old bridge need not be destroyed. It could be closed or even left open for limited traffic.

Caught short by the regulations they'd not read, local officials agreed to spare the bridge, a happy ending for all who know that grand old bridges, like the highway itself, are best appreciated when employed as they were intended.

Kansas and Route 66 have clung to one another since the highway was commissioned. Part of that is due to the fact that Kansas was dry for so long, and state officials were tough about it. In recent years, before state prohibition finally gave way, Kansas went to court to stop airlines from serving liquor over its airspace. The state lost.

But back in the harshest of the dry days, bootleggers gained a powerful hold in this little corner of Kansas because when escape was needed there were two getaway states close by. Agents could rarely close in before the bootleggers were warned by an elaborate system of lookouts and alarms. Worse for the lawmen, many stills were completely portable.

On one occasion—with only a few minutes' warning—there was only time for the alky cookers to dump everything and make a run for it. All their brew, mash, and stills went off Ryan's Bridge into the river below in one huge, illegal splash.

No one was arrested, since all the evidence had disappeared. Yet everyone in this part of the country knew where the stuff had been dumped. For as it happened, a flock of migrating geese were just downstream from the dumping. In an hour, they had taken on so much sour-mash cocktail that their flying ability dropped to near-zero.

Consequently, the geese made it only a little farther south. There, on the Route 66 bridge into Riverton, the whole flock of them—now absolutely plastered—ambled, honked, and staggered all over the bridge. The structure was narrow even for its day and vehicles had no room whatsoever to maneuver around the comical but now highly aggressive geese.

As their heads cleared the geese took to the skies again. And though their formation was ragged, the geese remembered Kansas as a place to have a good time. In subsequent years, the flock returned time and again to the waters below Ryan's Bridge—hoping, it would appear, for another free happy hour.

You never knew what might be lurking just out of sight along Oklahoma's old two-lanes. Holdups were commonplace and along some stretches, Route 66 was known as Robbers Road. Up around Commerce, though, life is more gently lived. The town is presently remembered as Mickey Mantle's birthplace. But it was almost known as Bonnie and Clyde's deathplace.

At the height of their unholy reign as America's most-wanted couple, Bonnie Parker and Clyde Barrow pulled a hasty job northeast of here. And their getaway road was good old Route 66—best highway west to anywhere.

The usual scenario was that Bonnie and Clyde would roll in, rob a bank or shoot up some one-cop town just for the sheer hell of it, and then go busting down the road with the law lagging far behind. This time, though, the lawmen employed a brand-new weapon in their war against crime—the telephone. Quick as sound, the cops could call ahead, flashing the word to Oklahoma. *Stop 'em, boys. They're headed your way.*

It would take a little time to prepare, but Commerce was the best place to set up an ambush for the two law-breakers. The advantage lay in two opposing ninety-

degree turns in Route 66 as the highway approaches
Commerce from the east. Even in their quick Ford V-8,
Bonnie and Clyde would be forced to slow almost to a
walk, and the lawmen would have the drop on 'em. Trouble
was, not much firepower was available in sleepy Ottawa
County. So the US military was called in.

The American government is always declaring war on
something, too often with Custeresque results. The liber-
als lost their War on Poverty and the conservatives have
certainly blown the War on Drugs. Still, lessons seem to
come hard to government types. For the War on Bonnie
and Clyde was declared right there in Commerce.

The army showed up with a heavy-caliber machine gun
and its best gunners. A sandbag emplacement was readied
in jiffy-quick time, and everyone scrunched down to
wait. And wait.

Bonnie and Clyde had apparently stopped somewhere,
raising a doubt about whether they would show up at all.
What if they took some side road? *Good God, they could be
in Arkansas by now.*

Suddenly, a car was spotted tearing in from the neigh-
boring town of Quapaw. Confirmation came quickly—it
was definitely Bonnie and Clyde. The machine-gun crew
was given the word to shoot the car to pieces and blow
'em away.

Angle and elevation were perfect as the lawbreakers'
car skittered around the first turn on two wheels. *Steady
now. Wait 'til they slow for the second turn.*

Safety off, the gunners traversed their target, waiting
for the order. Then it came . . . *FIRE!* A click was heard
and nothing else. The gun had jammed. Bonnie and Clyde,
now seeing the ambush that had been in store for them,
smiled sweetly and waved to all assembled. Then they tore
on through town, throttle wide open, heading for Texas
on Route 66.

This time no one phoned ahead.

Having regularly endured drought, flood, and famine it
was only a question of time until Oklahomans would be
called upon to face pestilence as well. And sure enough,
in the early 1940s, swarms of crickets moved in on Bristow. In a few days absolutely everything was covered with

them: screens, doors, plants, and fences. They came down chimneys and turned up in garden hoses. People swept them off the sidewalk almost hourly to allow customers to get to businesses without tromping through insect stew. All to no avail.

For a while, the popular Hamburger King restaurant persevered. They swept the place clean each morning—and hourly thereafter—while clearing crickets from pantries and grills. Still, the tide of battle favored the crickets.

One morning, a new addition went up under the sign that had always advertised the restaurant's World Famous Hamburger. Foreshadowing truth-in-advertising laws yet to come, it simply read: *Cricketburgers.*

A bit farther west, under the giant YUKON mill sign, Oklahoma's tradition of fair play in the face of the unexpected has always been most evident. The Yukon High School football team of 1943 was only one of two teams in the entire state that no other team had scored on over an entire season. Yukon also had a winning streak of thirty-four games in a row. So the folks in town knew how to rear and support a team. But it is not a tradition easily won.

Even before US 66 was routed through town, Yukon was working on fundamentals. In the early days, the school had neither equipment nor the money needed for a football program. So the merchants coughed up $100 for the team. The problem was that the money could buy pants or helmets but not both. Well, the team couldn't very well play in their skivvies, so the hundred bucks went for pants and the boys played bareheaded.

Real football shoes were a problem, too. But most players were able to make up for that by driving huge nails through their work shoes and playing barefoot during practice to avoid injuring their teammates.

The team's first game, with Geary High School, also on Route 66 for a time, was a tough one. Shoulder pads were nonexistent or were made up of old horse collars. Still, everything was going fairly well until a Yukon team member caught the ball, headed across the open field for the goal line—and disappeared.

For a moment the tiny crowd was stunned. Everyone

raced for the point at which the player had last been seen and found him stuck halfway down an open well that no one had noticed. He was pulled out safely by a team of horses, but a question remained about how to judge the action.

Some wanted to give the boy an automatic touchdown for his trouble. Others argued that he didn't deserve it since he'd been pulled out without being hurt all that badly. Still others insisted that the play be run over again.

After some heated discussion, the Yukon team was awarded half the distance to the goal line and next down. Everyone except the boy, who'd lost his shoes in the fall, was satisfied.

If the gods of football still hang out in Oklahoma, they must have thoroughly enjoyed that long-ago game between Yukon and Geary along old Route 66.

People in other states complain about the weather. Oklahomans collect it. And sometimes conditions were more than highway departments could deal with. So an experiment was tried while paving US 66 through Missouri and Oklahoma.

Quarter-round concrete lip-curbs were poured on either side of the roadway's main slab. It was hoped that the curbs would prevent erosion during hard rains. Highway engineers also said that the curbs would help direct wayward cars away from a dangerous soft shoulder.

The idea sounded reasonable but in the dipsy-doodle sections near Weatherford everything went wrong that could. During a hard rain, the curbs directed so much water onto the highway that the hilly sections looked like giant sluice boxes. And when the temperature dropped after a hard rain from the north, each paved hill turned into something like a vertical skating rink.

Truck drivers knew the roller-coaster road quite well, of course. But fearing they would lose traction near the top of a hill if their speed dropped too much—they went hell-for-breakfast down each grade.

A well-known clergyman was known for doing the same thing while on missions of spiritual importance, since he felt divinity so close at hand. A field engineer for the Oklahoma Highway Department recalls one frozen night when the clergyman and one of the wildest of the local truckers met practically on top of them.

Both the truck and the cleric's speeding flivver turned turtle on the spot—spreading, in quick succession, several hundred crates of frozen turnips and a Catholic priest across the icy highway.

No one turned out to be badly hurt and the priest returned to his parish house on foot to give serious thanksgiving. The road crew got back to work after doing their own *amens*. The turnips, apparently, passed directly on to veggie heaven.

Despite the trials of the Dust Bowl years, simple human kindness was in great supply. By contrast, our own recent recessions (no politician dares use the word *depression* today) have set new standards in meanness of spirit.

Yet back in the early 1930s, it was common for merchants to go all out for their customers during hard times. One Oklahoma native, now a retired school administrator, recalls that his father always carried the tenant cotton farmers who were his customers.

In 1929, those farmers were devastated when the price of cotton dropped to ten cents a pound. None of them could pay even a dime on their accounts. But the store owner was determined to see them through this one bad year. He sold off his own property, mortgaged the rest, and stayed in business. And at least a few farmers stayed on the land.

TEXAS

Some government officials, and a few cops in particular, always seem to have a way of overstepping their limits while pretending to serve the people. That's a common occurrence in big coastal cities, but it also happened at a famous night spot in Amarillo back in the 1950s. The Nat—originally a natatorium that was later boarded over to become a ballroom—drew many of the top bands and performers after reopening in 1926.

Just a few doors from Route 66, the Nat was perfectly located for one-night stands by all the great names touring the country. Paul Whiteman, Benny Goodman, and Harry James all played here. But by the mid-1950s, big bands were out. It cost too much to keep them on the road, and except for the college-prom circuit, most disappeared from sight. Helping them into early retirement were the new solo acts with small groups of three or four sidemen. Rock and Roll was hot, Country & Western was on the move—and the music was cheap.

Buddy Holly could be had for not much more than room and board and Willie Nelson was still working the honky-tonks while he wrote great songs that no one would let him record. Even the King was working the

small rooms and out-of-the-way places. Of course, that
didn't last long, and eventually audiences would pay more
for a single rock group than for a dozen swing bands.

That's about the time Little Richard was booked into
the Nat. As soon as word got around, threats began to fil-
ter into the owner—not from offended citizens—but
from law-enforcement officials, people charged with
knowing better. The Nat's owner wouldn't stand for in-
timidation, however, and stated flatly that Little Richard
would go on as planned.

The sticking point was the posturing that the performer was known to do on stage. Lewd and lascivious
conduct, the sheriff said it was. Everybody else said it was
great. Most thought nothing of the threat of arrest. Just
Smokeys blowin' smoke. Elvis Presley's act was far more
suggestive, and it was hard to top (or even classify) what
Jerry Lee Lewis did on stage. About all anyone could say
is that he ended his shows with most of his clothes still on,
even if he sometimes burned the piano. By comparison,
Little Richard might not be a garden-club act, but he was
well within accepted limits for the High Plains.

The real trouble, of course, was that Little Richard was
black. And that was what really got him busted that night
at the Nat. Roughed up and hauled away in cuffs before
doing *anything,* the performer was slapped with a stiff fine
and escorted to the city limits. Today, the story is still regularly told to Route 66 travelers. That's a good way, the
people here believe, to keep present lawmen on notice
that it would be better if something like this did not happen again.

Some men naturally combine business ability and show-
manship. Far fewer men also create the air of gentle
toughness it takes to create something of great value for
the community, in spite of hard times. Cal Farley was one
of those few.

A wrestling champion and semi-pro baseball player,
Cal always seemed to be in the thick of things. Soon after
the Amarillo Gassers folded as a baseball team, he took
over a failing tire shop and established one of the first traditions on fledgling Route 66—the Wun-Stop-Duzzit. Its
name, plus the convenience of Amarillo's first, got the

business off to a good start. It was often said that a traveler far from home always got the same price as a local buyer. But it was the owner's gift for capturing the imagination that spelled success. Cal Farley was a natural-born promoter. And he had nerve.

At a time when Amarillo's oil boom was dwindling, new tires weren't a high priority with folks on the High Plains. Yet Cal wanted to demonstrate the clear superiority of the BF Goodrich product he carried. He knew the tires were tough but he needed to make new customers out of disbelievers. So Cal hired a pilot and a sleek monoplane, ready to prove how rough-and-ready his tires were. In the press and on the radio, he announced that he would toss a mounted and inflated tire out of the airplane at an altitude of no less than 2,700 feet.

Now that would be a fair distance for one of today's tires. In 1929, when tire failures were as common as table salt, they might as well be dropped from the moon. But Cal had faith in his product and carried on even as the side-betting favored his opponent.

On the appointed day, at a field where a white target-circle had been painted, dust rose from the cars—hundreds of them—that brought Texans from every direction to witness the event. Cal's hired plane took off and traffic on every nearby road stopped. Finally, after the plane had circled the field enough to be sure of everyone's attention, a mounted tire flew from the open doorway, heading straight down for the target. It hit with a helluva thump, bounced a couple of hundred feet into the air, and came to rest undamaged. Cal's point was made: these are really tough tires and we sell 'em. The Amarillo *Daily News* gave Cal Farley's promotional event most of the front page. Business soared.

To keep things moving right along, Cal also ran his own live radio show from the Wun-Stop-Duzzit, and planned other stunts, like having his lowest-ranking salesmen ride donkeys in a parade through downtown.

But the Depression was deepening, times were getting tougher, and the number of abandoned youngsters on Amarillo's streets grew daily. Most had already been arrested for petty theft of food and clothing, and the rate of serious crime among young boys was rising.

If others could ignore the problem or postpone it with jail sentences, Cal could not. He knew kids from his days as a baseball player, he understood their needs and their terrors, and he knew something needed to be done. But it had to be more than a momentary stunt. Somehow these kids had to be unplugged from their city-street lives and given a fresh start out on the land. Cal Farley labored and hustled and jawboned.

And in 1939, on the steps of a crumbling courthouse in the ghost town of Old Tascosa, Cal Farley accepted on behalf of thousands of boys he would come to know, a grant of 120 acres to be called Boys Ranch. The first staff members came from Elk City, Oklahoma. The boys came from everywhere. Three youngsters were even put on a bus by their destitute mother with tags that read "Deliver to Boys Ranch, Amarillo, Texas." A movie was made by MGM. The boys kept coming.

The Wun-Stop-Duzzit eventually became a department store with the same reputation for variety and fairness as the original Route 66 business. And Boys Ranch is still going strong, with an additional 3,000 acres and close to 500 residents.

There are other stories of love and wisdom to be found along the old highway, but none with greater accomplishment.

NEW MEXICO

When weather can't seem to make it all the way east to Texas or Oklahoma, it just naturally drops in on Tucumcari. In fact, that's how the town got started in the first place.

At the turn of the century, two men were stranded at Six Shooter Siding by a mean-spirited, three-week snowstorm. After a round of true hospitality, they just happened to mention that a railroad would be coming through. Land was snapped up, and when the railroad made Six Shooter Siding a regular stop, Tucumcari was born. Twenty-five years later Highway 66 was routed along that same railroad easement and Tucumcari became the town of 1,000 motel rooms.

With Route 66 bringing carloads of people into Tucumcari every day, there was bound to be a mystery or two. The most baffling turned out to be the Matchbook Murder, ultimately solved by the Sheriff of Quay County, Claude Monkus.

In 1951, a body was found by an itinerant bottle-picker three miles west of town. Yet there wasn't a single clue about who the victim was or how he came to be there. Only that someone had taken the trouble to shoot him five times.

Through fingerprints, Sheriff Claude located the victim's family in Ohio and obtained a description, along with the useful information that the man had been headed for California. Shortly thereafter, the victim's car turned up on an impound lot in Amarillo, bereft of any other clues, but bearing a matchbook from The Hitching Post in Sturgeon Bay, Wisconsin.

Armed with only that much, the sheriff began tracking the victim and his killer. After checking in with every gas station and motel as far east as Shamrock, a description was eventually obtained of a hitchhiker seen in the victim's company. And sure enough, the owner of The Hitching Post recognized a former fry cook from Sheriff Claude's telephone description and remembered that the fellow quit to head for California.

An all-points bulletin went out on the murderer and some months later a young deputy in Northern California's redwood country arrested him. The trial in Tucumcari was brief, the verdict was *guilty*, and the matchbook murderer paid the price.

Sheriff Claude later received an award from his fellow peace officers in the tristate area, and in 1965 was honored as Peace Officer of the Month by *Master Detective Magazine*. No computers, no technicalities over DNA samples, just good old-fashioned police work and a single matchbook found along Route 66.

Wilmer and his sidekick Woofie were inveterate watchers. In fact, there were probably none better in the state of New Mexico. The two lived just west of Santa Rosa and always turned out to watch one of the state's two or three snowplows whenever a blizzard rolled in. And they measured carefully the progress of any roadwork.

So when Route 66 was finally graded and paved on a line straight west of Santa Rosa toward Albuquerque, the boys had something special to scrutinize. A great deal of watching was needed, too, especially around Tijeras Canyon, which had stumped roadbuilders for years. The route through the canyon to Albuquerque was so torturous, with so many rock outcroppings to be cleared, that the blasting went on for months.

Not long after they began serious watching of the

blasting work—from an exceptionally safe distance—Wilmer and Woofie noticed something about the way in which the highway was being built. Instead of the steel forms they'd seen on another job or two, the Route 66 crews were using wooden forms nailed up from two-by-tens.

What's more, and this was the interesting part to Wilmer and Woofie, the wood was being constantly replaced with new stock. Around nightfall, as the job shut down, the two-by-tens that had been used that day were stacked neatly by the construction shack and the wood from the previous day was loaded onto a flatbed truck and hauled away.

Back at their cabin, Woofie opined that the Tijeras job was using a hell of a lot of new two-by-tens and that the old stock was certainly going somewhere. Wilmer agreed and the two invested in a long-distance telephone call to the Bernalillo County highway office. *Were there any other construction jobs nearby to watch?* they wanted to know. *No, nothing more than repair work. Sorry.*

The boys thanked their informant, gave the long-distance operator the rest of their nickels, and figured they were definitely onto a profitable item. Winter would be coming on soon and they had no stovewood, except for some green piñon that smoked something terrible and put out precious little heat.

But they did have a good crossbuck saw that could cut through those two-by-tens in nothing flat. A little hatchet work after that and they'd have enough stove kindling to last until the end of February at least.

Next morning Woofie and Wilmer skipped their usual breakfast at the White Cottage Cafe and headed straight for the job site. There they spent most of the day making sure they knew who the players were. Wilmer was pretty sure that the fellow standing over by the shack—who never got his hands dirty and nodded a lot whenever any of the crew spoke to him—was the foreman. But they wanted to take no chances by asking. So they put in another two days of watching, just to be sure.

Finally, they made their move. Sidling up to the foreman, Woofie began passing the time of day. It was hard going, too. The old guy was intent on the job and not very talkative. Woofie's chatter didn't seem welcome. So Wilmer, always the man with a friendly word, stepped in and went to work on the foreman. Once in a while, one of the construction crew would drive by in a truck giving a wave. And all three men would wave back. By day's end, Wilmer and Woofie felt like they were part of the crew.

Things progressed fairly well after that and Woofie picked up a pint of expensive sour-mash whiskey for the foreman—as a token of friendship, you might say. Apparently he'd even got the right brand because the foreman seemed quite pleased by the gesture. Another day and another pint, this time from Wilmer, and the time seemed right to pop the question. *Would anyone mind if we stopped by tonight and picked up a few of those two-by-tens?*

The foreman said nothing, just stared at the frosted ground, shaking his head slightly. Woofie knew instantly that they had come up short and beat a hasty retreat, leaving Wilmer to put a little friendliness back into the negotiations. In due time, Woofie was back with a whole fifth of the very agreeable sour-mash whiskey.

That certainly seemed to do the trick. Another word or two and the foreman nodded. *Sure, nobody would notice a few missing two-by-tens. Help yourselves.*

That night Wilmer and Woofie had piled nearly all the wood into an old pickup with bad springs when a deputy sheriff rolled up in his black Ford. This time the negotiations were short and sweet. Woofie explained that they were just unloading a bunch of two-by-tens—as a personal contribution to the good work being done by the road crew. *It's our patriotic duty,* Wilmer told the deputy.

Woofie was more straightforward. He wanted to know if it was the booze-guzzling foreman who'd ratted out on them. The question puzzled the deputy. As it turned out he'd just happened by with no crime-fighting on his mind at all. And the foreman? Well, the deputy explained, the job's foreman was down with the crew supervising all the blasting, just like always.

Then who was that fella up by the construction shack? the boys wanted to know. And that put a stitch into the deputy. Between belly laughs he told the pair that the old guy they'd been buying sour-mash whiskey for was another sidewalk supervisor——a full-time watcher just like themselves. Wilmer and Woofie were so stricken by the news that the deputy told them to keep some of the two-by-tens still on the pickup.

Hell, someone else was stealing them anyway.

For most early travelers on Route 66 through the South-west, the only continuing fact of life other than the high-way itself was the Santa Fe Railway. On a two-lane where hours of solitude could pass without sight of another ve-hicle——or even a line of telephone poles to mark the dis-tance, there was little contrast or relief from creeping boredom. Especially for backseat kids.

Oh, there were the steep-sided arroyos along the high-way, where a sign reading DIP marked the point at which the family car would become completely airborne at any speed over 55. Those were always good for a little excitement.

The rest of the traveling day was quartered into times when the silver-sided *Chief* or *Super Chief* came tearing through. Easily hitting 90 miles per hour on some straight stretches, the Santa Fe streamliners in their red-yellow-silver paint schemes hissed by at such a rate that passen-gers' faces were only a blur.

But if each train encounter was a major event of the day for Route 66 travelers, the streamliners also marked the end of a lucrative trade in Indian blankets carried on at de-pots across the West. By the late 1940s, the trains were stopping in fewer cities, and then only briefly. Not enough time for passengers to appreciate the wares, or to buy.

Soon the blanket merchants moved on over to roadside souvenir stands along Route 66. It wasn't the same, though. One Navajo woman, who worked with her weaver-mother outside the Fred Harvey Alvarado Hotel in Albuquerque, remembers that train passengers were more considerate and less inclined to haggle over small amounts than tourists on the highway. She also recalls how Anglo merchants at the depot began hurting the trade by hiring Pueblo Indians to sell cheap blankets——made in Brooklyn——for much less.

For a time, the daughter tried to even the score by

telling customers that the competition sold blankets that were transported by diseased people. That's why the goods were so much cheaper. When her mother learned of this, she was both angered and amused, so the girl was scolded in good humor. Nevertheless, machine-made blanket sales increased and the Navajos soon moved on.

For years, all that remained of their presence was the little Navajo boy whose image appeared in Santa Fe advertising. In the end even that disappeared as an undesirable stereotype, along with the passenger service of which the Santa Fe Railway was once so proud.

West of Albuquerque, along the older thirty-two-mile stretch of highway from Los Lunas to Correo, there was little action other than double-headed Santa Fe freights and the railway's sleek streamliners. The rest was—and still is—New Mexican arroyos, scrub, and sky. So travelers were more than ready for a stop at Dan's Bar, Cafe, and Motel. And they often got more than they expected.

Dan's was one of the original last-chance operations. Except in place of two-headed rattlesnakes, the place featured a midget bull and Katy the Dancing Bear. Although it was true that Katy could do a few steps, her real interest lay in hustling the tourists for drinks, and she was very good at it. Some even said that Katy could read the labels, because she clearly knew the difference between soft drinks and beer—which she would always choose at any distance, and could drain faster than a chug-a-lug champ.

This same section of Route 66 was also a favorite haunt of New Mexico State Policemen who needed relief from a relentless desert sun and the loneliness of patrol. In the 1950s, just before Correo was bypassed by the new Albuquerque cutoff, Dan's was also a hotbed of illicit competition between the highway patrolmen, who were running pursuit-model Fords, and Dan's employees, who favored the hot new Buick Centurys. Somehow, when they caught sight of one another on a straight stretch, the checkered flag just naturally dropped, with the Buick going two for three. Though the participants were never found out, you could always tell from the smell of burned oil coming from a pair of cars parked out front—along with windshields made opaque by sacrificial bugs—that the boys had been at it again.

Correo is gone now, with virtually no remains. But if you listen for the sound of racing exhausts on the wind, and keep an eye out for classic muscle cars, you won't be disappointed. GTOs, hot Fords, and Trans Ams still populate this stretch of highway, often driven by officers of the court, no less, looking for a little action out on Route 66.

Not many along old Route 66 knew of the Singing House. Fewer speak of it today. It is one of those stories of the heart that could suffer at the hands of strangers and is not often repeated. But there is a spot, hidden from view, west of Laguna and north toward the Continental Divide, and it is there that the house once stood.

No one knows where the builders came from, exactly. Somewhere near Ft. Smith, Arkansas, they say: a hardworking but frail man and his handsome wife, driven out by the dust and hard times of the 1930s. Picking up Route 66 in Oklahoma City, the couple made it to Santa Rosa before their ancient Willys gave out. Too expensive to fix, they traded it for a clapped-out Reo and struggled into Albuquerque before it, too, died a junker's death.

Now the wife, it is said, had a voice as sweet as sunlight on the dew. She'd sung since her school days at a country church and had even been approached by talent agents. But she wanted nothing to do with the commerce of music.

Still, when the last of their money was gone and her husband was ill from walking the city in search of an honest day's labor, the wife had a change of heart. Dressing in her best, she went from one place to another, until she found a clubowner who would hear her. As the club's small band fell in behind the simple melodies she sang, the room hushed. Her voice, with its transparent quality, compelled attention and sold extra drinks. The clubowner knew a voice of gold when he heard it and hired the woman on the spot.

Soon she had become the most popular singer in the valley. Yet, even with more than enough money to move on, her husband recovered slowly. He was, you see, not working. And that fact sapped whatever strength he found in himself.

The clear New Mexico air agreed with him, though, and his color was better than his wife could remember. He'd also taken up whittling again, rendering in soft, piney detail the small desert animals he'd seen along the edges of the city.

So one Sunday morning his wife said what was on her mind. Why not build a home in the high country just to the west? He was handy and could do much of the work himself. She could finish out her scheduled performances and help him. Perhaps they could even find a market for his carvings. Surprisingly, her husband took to the idea and they found a perfect building site, plus two Pueblo Indians who were wizards with adobe.

Nearly every day, as the work progressed, the wife would sing to her husband and the workmen and to the house itself, while she labored alongside them. When the house was finished, the sound of her voice seemed to have become a part of every brick and board. Indeed, in the afternoon breezes, windows opened on opposite sides of the house brought a sweet trilling that rose and fell, changing its timbre with the wind. Neighbors from small homesteads nearby heard of the house and often stopped by just to hear its song. The man and his wife were obliging but not encouraging. It was a private thing, they felt.

With their house safely up before the first winter storm, the husband drove off one morning with samples of his work to show owners of souvenir shops along the highway. He was more confident now; everyone who'd seen his carvings wanted to buy and his work would surely sell well once the Depression ended. With a snug house and a great many of his carvings put by, the future looked bright.

Accounts differ about what happened next, of course, as accounts always do. Some say the wife was trying to save her husband's carvings from a flash fire that engulfed their home. Others say the fire was set by intruders. There was no real evidence one way or the other. The husband only knew that his wife had perished, and after a few disconsolate weeks, the man wandered off alone, disappearing without a trace.

Only four sentinel corners of adobe bricks remain. Even the charred roof timbers have been carried away for firewood.

Yet here is a strange thing. Occasional visitors to the site swear that the sweet voice embodied in the house can still be heard. Inexplicably, it is clearest on a day when there is no wind at all. The almost-transparent tones do not come, it is said, from the adobe pillars, nor from anything that can be found in the ruins. The soft trilling is simply there, in the clear New Mexico air, just above the rock and weathered grasses. As if it had always been so, here, along the western rift of America.

Crooks never had much of a chance on Route 66 through the West. Many, from scam artists to killers, traveled the road but little crime was actually committed along its path. That's not due to any gentling effect of the highway, however.

Instead, the low crime rate is because most towns only have one major thoroughfare—Route 66. It's the way into town and the only way out. No choice of north or south or back-alley places to hide. Commit a crime here; stay here.

In Gallup, Nechero's Texaco station has only been robbed once in fifty-three years of service to Route 66 travelers. Gallup is too small to hole up in, and once out of town there's just nowhere to go. Faced with the Great Empty to the west, one crook raced back into town, only to be stuck behind the Inter-Tribal Indian Ceremonial Parade. When the parade passed by the police cruiser at the far end of town, the cops simply pulled the robber from his car and tossed him in the hoosegow.

The parade itself has always been held on a Saturday in August, and it's a three-hour lulu. It is such a big deal, in fact, that when Highway 66 was first routed through Gallup, a special exemption was required. You see, US numbered highways were supposed to remain open no matter what. But not in Gallup. Here, the parade came first.

Well, it took a while for federal and state planners to accustom themselves to that idea, but they finally took it gracefully. And for over six decades, traffic halted on

Route 66 while dancers, drummers, riders, and towns-people celebrated the Native American heritage to which the town owes a large part of its culture, art, and livelihood.

Today, New Mexico has a well-deserved reputation as a movie-making center. Hollywood productions began making films in Las Vegas twenty-five years before Route 66 made an appearance, when crews and equipment traveled only by train. Las Vegas boasted excellent rail connections. The city also offered first-rate accommodations for cast members at Fred Harvey's La Castaneda Hotel, with a pretty fair nightlife to boot.

Albuquerque also managed to attract a little of the movie action in those early years. But the biggest burst of movie-making energy was centered in Gallup. And not by accident. Stars of the 1940s and '50s like Erroll Flynn, Spencer Tracy, Virginia Mayo, Robert Mitchum, Gene Tierney, and Kirk Douglas were in part lured to Gallup by a well-appointed watering hole that was already legendary among Hollywood's elite—El Rancho Hotel.

The place was comfortable enough for Mayo's entourage, and spacious enough for Flynn who typically rode his horse right on through the lobby and straight into the bar. Even today, the place holds an uncanny power of attraction.

El Rancho's rooms are also named for the stars who stayed in them. And therein lies a tale. At a time when Hollywood had a reputation for wild parties and outrageous behavior, studios were unwilling to acknowledge that their stars were even traveling together, much less romantically involved. And the gossip columnists had been busy linking Spencer Tracy—quite accurately as it happened—with Katharine Hepburn.

When location work on *Sea of Grass* was begun in Gallup, it was carefully announced through the press that Tracy and Hepburn were not present. Yet many recall seeing them together around El Rancho at the time, and the rooms still bearing their names are right next door to one another. So where does life end and a legend begin?

Mike Pitel of the New Mexico Tourism Department wondered the same thing. So he did a little undercover research at El Rancho, figuring that Spencer and Kate were getting by, despite pressure from studio executives. Perhaps, even after all these years, there still might be a clue.

There was. When Pitel and a co-investigator rented the Tracy and Hepburn rooms for a night, they discovered—in the farthest reaches of a closet along the adjoining wall—a flimsy hardboard panel tacked in place and easily removed. It was all that separated the two rooms. El Rancho had aided in the triumph of love over public relations.

Historically, western New Mexico and northern Arizona have been competitors. But the people of both states were united in helping the Dust Bowl refugees headed west. In a steady stream they came, Okies mostly, but Arkies and Georgia Crackers, too—their land broken or just plain gone.

On they came. For those who'd begun the journey with old trucks and cut-down cars, the grades beyond Albuquerque took their toll. Ruined hulks of the refugees' pitiful machines were scattered all along Route 66, as were their graves.

Roadsiders generally had little more than the refugees themselves. Some merchants even conspired to sell spoiled food, faulty auto parts, and bad tires. Even tap water carried a price often beyond measure. Gas was a few cents a gallon. Water for a thirsty infant could run fifty cents a pint. So Dust Bowlers learned to take their water from the creek beds, free—until some black hearts began poisoning the waters.

By the mid-1930s, countless thousands of those on the road knew they had no hope at all of getting through on their own. Everything they had ever owned was gone.

Finally, when certain starvation faced the travelers, people along the roadside pitched in with everything they could find. Tourist courts in New Mexico gave free clothing and food to children. Doctors along the border delivered and mended as best they could, buying medicine on what little credit they had left.

This outpouring of love is one of the most remarkable things to come out of that period, gracing Route 66 in a way nothing else could. For long after the thin trails of homeless families had crossed into California, the refugee remembered their debts. When there was finally enoug to make it through each day, they began sending what they could to the people who had helped them. In nickels and dimes and worn half-dollars, it was sent—month after month—to the Samaritans of Route 66.

Today, there is a small society of families made up of roadsiders and the refugees they befriended. A bond spanning sixty-some years still connects those long-ago travelers with people from Grants, Thoreau, Gallup, Lupton, Allantown, Holbrook, and Winslow. Letters and snapshots of children and grandchildren are exchanged, and holidays are spent together as human kindness during those terrible times is still honored.

ARIZONA

Unlike some towns along the highway, Winslow has little in the way of local curses—and doesn't want any. It is often difficult enough to accomplish something here without interference from the netherworld. Townfolks work hard, take their pleasures as they can, and keep track of the traffic on Route 66. Sometimes that's plenty.

In fact, the only occasion when traffic was halted on Route 66 occurred in the 1940s. A local pub owner faced the problem of moving his solid, thirty-foot bar across the highway to a new location. The bar had been custom-built right inside Bus & Bill's Bar, so it would be a shame to break it up just for a trip across the street.

Yet, as the bar stood—huge, cumbersome, and glued to the floor by its own tonnage—no moving company would touch the job for less than a second mortgage. At length, after everything else had been moved, Bus put out the word: *Grand Closing! Free Beer at 4 P.M. Sharp!* Small boys circulated a stack of handmade posters among the town's most cost-conscious elbow-benders.

An offer of free money couldn't have attracted more able-bodied regulars in this parched high-desert community. At the appointed hour, Winslow's stoutest menfolk stood shoulder to shoulder along the heavy wooden structure at Bus & Bill's. And after several rounds, Bus announced his intention. The bar would now be moved across the street.

Bus's patrons gave it their best. Holding longnecks in one hand and a length of bar in the other, they all faced north, grunted, lifted, and strained. The bar, now looking like a crippled mahogany centipede of monstrous proportions, wobbled slowly through the front door and out onto Route 66.

But the need for relief was evident, so Bus made another announcement. It was definitely time to take a break. And the moving crew had certainly earned it. With a great, scraping *crumph*, the bar teetered and came to rest at the exact midpoint of America's busiest transcontinental highway, bringing traffic to a complete stop.

The din made by horns of cars and trucks must have been deafening. But the boys would not be hurried. Another round of free beer was served and amiably discussed. Finally, accompanied by sounds of pure-malt satisfaction, the bar made its way to the other side of the highway.

Some years later, as the story still recirculates around town, many have expressed an interest in preserving the moment. A small memorial plaque was considered for a time. But the best suggestion was to place a standard yellow-diamond caution sign at the spot. In honor of one of the few times Route 66 was ever closed to traffic, the sign would read: **SLOW BAR XING.**

Travelers along Route 66 have always been highly regarded by towns and businesses along the way. But the turkey award usually went to the big-city tourists—demanding types who sneered at local customs.

Still, Route 66 can be a great equalizer and for many Easterners, the trip west could be arduous off the road as well as on it. Some roadside businesspeople, especially on slow days, were even known to lay in wait for the self-absorbed and incautious. One who did was the concessionaire at Meteor Crater.

Rimmy Jim ran the combined trading post, chat-and-chew filling station, and liquor store that bore his name. A former cattle baron who'd been run to ground by rustlers over the years, Rimmy Jim had learned to take life one day at a time, usually accompanied by a heavy dose of humor. With a ten-gallon hat that he wore with the fore brim turned down like a dress fedora, Rimmy Jim played a novel, hybrid role that was part cowboy, part Ernest Hemingway.

Locals loved the show, and from his vantage point on the crater rim, the canny shopkeeper carefully watched the cars out on Route 66. When someone whose car he recognized didn't stop for coffee when headed up to Flagstaff in the morning, he'd charge them double when they stopped in for a cup on the way back. And over the years, he kept up a series of running gags with just about everyone in the region.

Rimmy Jim had only two sore spots: salesmen and snooty Eastern ladies. He dealt with the salesmen by offering to bury them free if they even stepped foot in his place.

Most, seeing the wild look in Rimmy Jim's eye, skedaddled without even leaving their automobiles. The fact that there were some headstones randomly placed just out back probably hastened their departures.

Rimmy took a little more time with Eastern female tourists, however. It was a long way between rest stops in those days and people often drove in just to use the facilities.

There was some primitive indoor plumbing for paying customers at Rimmy Jim's place. But when he spied an ample lady with Eastern airs, Rimmy invariably sent her on to the outhouse several yards removed from the storefront. Once the lady had time to be adequately enthroned there, a voice from a secret loudspeaker would issue from the deepest recesses below the seat.

In pleading tones, Rimmy would ask the woman to move over to the second hole since he hadn't finished painting the underside of the first one yet.

Most everyone in northern Arizona was in on the joke and locals would often drop by just for the regular sight of matronly forms exploding from the outhouse door in total disarray.

There are plenty of rest stops and trading posts along

Route 66 these days, and Meteor Crater is still open for business. But there will never be another place like Rimmy Jim's. All those who knew him regret the passing of that time, and what he brought to the highway and all those who loved it.

There's not much left at Two Guns, just east of Flagstaff. And it may be just as well. For the place is said to be cursed, with death or financial disarray in store for anyone who occupies this place.

The sorry history of Two Guns began with the slaughter of fifty Navajo men, women, and children by Apache raiders from the White Mountains to the east. After a second raid, the Apaches vanished, but were later discovered by Navajo trackers to be hiding in a cave at Canyon Diablo, the present-day site of Two Guns. Caught in their underground hideout, with no chance for escape, the Apaches were eventually smoked to death by fires set at the cave's entrance by the Navajos. Since then the site has been considered sacred by both Nations. Only a few outlaws ever frequented the place, and to a man, they got their tickets punched by pursuers.

By the time a forerunner of Route 66 spanned the formidable Canyon Diablo in the early 1920s, a lodge and post office had been established. This, despite Indian warnings that warrior spirits roamed the canyon, often in the form of mountain lions. The property owner was one of many who ignored those warnings—and never lived to reap the tourist rewards he'd planned on. In 1926, when Highway 66 was officially routed through Two Guns, he was brutally murdered and his store burned to the ground.

Now you'd think that plans to commercialize the death cave would die with him. But a new owner turned up and pressed on with the project. Again ignoring Indian warnings, he cleared the cave of its relics and used the skulls of the fallen Apache warriors as decorations. Then, in the ultimate nose-thumbing, he built cages out behind his gas station and there put captured mountain lions on display to the tourist trade.

Within months, the would-be showman was clawed

and nearly cut in half by two of the creatures. Shortly after that, his daughter was killed in a freak accident on the highway and the man left for good.

Two Guns opened and closed again several times over the years, but the site was too attractively situated on Route 66 to stay empty for long. Another owner stepped in, and for a time, it did quite well. But in 1971 the place mysteriously blew up. Everything was destroyed, except the lions' cages and a few rock walls.

A newer gas station and campground, off the original site, have since opened and closed. And in the early 1990s, another new owner took possession, had impressive photographs of himself taken, and promised great things for Two Guns. He even put up a small fee to have the curse lifted, but the Indian medicine man knew he was being underpaid by a wealthy promoter and left the curse in place. After a series of unhappy incidents, that owner put the place up for sale.

If you're a betting person, the odds favoring history are now about eight to one.

One of the last towns along Route 66 in Arizona to catch the fever of highway revival, Flagstaff is now solidly aboard. And the Museum Club has been a leader in preserving the mood of the road's glory days.

Formerly called the Zoo Club in deference to all the animal heads hung on its walls, the place recalls the while-you-wait taxidermist who originally practiced here, and predates Route 66 by over a decade.

Built in 1915, the exterior has changed very little over the years and is a testament to log construction. Inside, the club is pure wild-west saloon, with an arched bar and supporting pillars furnished by the five trees around which the place was built. Indeed, if Annie Oakley and Teddy Roosevelt got together to design a bar, this is what it would look like. Absolutely bang-bully.

The club has had its share of fame and misfortune, too. Although it gained an early reputation as a playpen for local rowdies, it was later transformed by a new owner. Live music became the mainstay, with the likes of Waylon and Willie playing here, along with assorted local bands.

Everything was looking up when the owner's lovely, dark-haired wife fell to her death from the club's staircase; he took his own life soon after.

Exactly the stuff of ghost stories, right? And the club has since had several encounters of the harrowing kind, but none of these centered on the double tragedy as might be expected.

Instead, the accounts are of a young, blonde woman with crystal-green eyes who has been appearing or making her presence felt here since the late 1950s. Over the years, the woman has ordered drinks, only to disappear; lit wood fires in the great hearth after closing time; and left chairs rocking in the empty club. Moans of pleasure have also been heard in a vacant upstairs apartment.

Credibility has been added to these reports by a live-in manager who was actually pinned to his bed—control your fantasies here, guys—by the blonde, who clearly intended him anything but harm. That manager bailed out a second-story window, rolled down the roof below, and still shaking, called the present owner from a nearby pay phone. Pausing only to clothe himself, he then left town and hasn't been back since.

So who could this wandering spirit be? Just another disembodied soul, with no connection to Route 66 or the club? Seems unlikely, doesn't it? After all, whatever spirit world exists would certainly be governed by certain natural laws, however unfamiliar to us.

Ghosts, like their physical counterparts, do not appear to operate randomly in the universe. Some, bent on a trip along Route 66, might have migrated here from Carthage, Missouri, with no trouble at all. If you happen to be in the Museum Club around closing time, you may have cause to consider the possibilities.

For now, it is enough to speculate about what the lady might prefer in the way of a drink. An extra glass ordered at a secluded corner booth? Sure, why not?

During World War II, a gunnery school for bomber crews was located right along Route 66, on the site of the present airport, east of town. Many of the wartime structures are still there.

After the war, Kingman's base became one of the first

aircraft boneyards. As Storage Depot 41, the field took in bombers and fighters from our forces around the world. At one point, over 7,000 surplus aircraft were dumped here by the War Assets Administration. Finally, someone asked what was going to be done with it all.

At first, the government tried to sell the aircraft off singly and in small lots. But there aren't a lot of uses for B-17s and dive bombers in peacetime, and the scrap aluminum market was more than depressed by the surplus—it was nonexistent. Mind you, bombers were even being flown in with full tanks, directly from the factories that were still producing them after the war's end.

All of which prompted a local businessman to step forward. He offered to take all that junk off the government's hands and melt it down for little more than his cost. The government, nearly desperate in a political year, even helped out with a grant, wondering, no doubt, what desert turnip truck the fellow could have fallen from.

Not long after, a routine inspection tour by federal auditors revealed our entrepreneur's secret. He was indeed handing off the scrap metal for virtually nothing—but he was making a fortune by selling the aviation gas left in the fuel tanks of every arriving aircraft.

And you were wondering how federal toilet seats could possibly cost several thousand dollars.

During the early part of World War II, with terrible losses for America in the Pacific, everyone's attention was on survival. Survival in combat, survival of relationships, survival crossing the country—and the desert, especially—with wornout cars, bald tires, and heavily rationed fuel.

Yet for one courageous young bride, the highway offered the shortest, perhaps only, route to her husband's side. An Army Air Corps pilot, he was assigned to a special new task group to be formed in Florida and flew there directly, after the briefest of honeymoons.

Many road maps were both poor and outdated, what with no new printings and most of the cartographers drafted for military duty. It was the same with the highways themselves—little or no maintenance and detours appearing everywhere, some for the duration.

So the bride did her best. It was important that she see her new husband again, before the war took him away. She tried to call several times, to let him know she was coming, but communications with the new group were blacked out.

Setting out from the West Coast, she followed Route 66 as far as Oklahoma City, then continued east through Ft. Smith to Eglin Field in Florida. But by the time she arrived, the group had already been transferred to another base and everything was totally hush-hush.

Wives have a way of knowing when the chips are really down and the young bride kept her spirits up in the face of no news at all about her husband or his group's mission.

The news finally broke. Doolittle's Raiders had flown Army bombers off the aircraft carrier *Hornet* and bombed Japan, our first effort in turning the tide. Her husband had been one of the wounded, but surviving, pilots. Their story later became part of an MGM movie about the raid and its effect on the crew's lives.

The young bride was Ellen Lawson and her husband was Lieut. Ted Lawson, pilot of the seventh B-25 in Jimmy Doolittle's raid and subject of the best-selling book, *Thirty Seconds Over Tokyo*. And later, a town on Route 66 in Missouri renamed itself Doolittle, in honor of the raid's leader and the courage of all the men who took part.

It's often the fashion of some of today's writers to make a show of themselves and their work. Perhaps their egos would shrivel without the attention. Yet the granddaddy of all Route 66 authors was not like that. Though he later received both the Pulitzer and Nobel prizes for literature, John Steinbeck remained unassuming, private, and passionately devoted to his work. He also cared deeply for the migrant workers he knew from his own days of laboring in the fields.

Virtually no one recalls the author's tour of Route 66 as he worked on *The Grapes of Wrath*, writing as many as 2,000 words a day—in longhand—as he traveled the highway, patiently building his story of the Joads' flight to California. In his journal, Steinbeck lamented his work, believing it was not very good. A run-of-the-mill book, he thought, though the world soon came to know better.

Arizona sections of Route 66 appear during a montage sequence in John Ford's film production of Steinbeck's masterpiece. Shots of the highway along the California border give great depth to the feeling of being on the road during those Dust Bowl Days.

Along the Colorado River shore at Needles, where the temperature is often epic, is a place where Steinbeck waded into the river to escape the heat. Later, realizing the power of giving oneself to the waters, the novelist wrote of the Joad menfolk doing the same thing. It is a simple moment in the story, yet Steinbeck's compassion and plain words help confer upon all of us our humanity.

CALIFORNIA

It is in the nature of a free people to take independence for granted. Which leads us to complain about the federal government and the justice system from time to time. And both are flawed. So are we. It all comes with the territory.

But the Great Depression of the 1930s still reminds us that freedom is always subject to the personal fears of those in power. It can disappear in a flash. And even if recovered, it can be a hard thing to get people to talk about afterward.

Take our freedom to cross state lines whenever we wish, for example. We think nothing of it today. Yet, during the Depression, it was a close-run thing—especially along the California border.

You see, California more than any other state was isolated by its mountains and deserts from the rest of the country until well after World War II. Simple things like cars and major appliances were manufactured within the state because transportation costs from the East were too high. Long-haul trucking was almost unknown and the Santa Fe Railway had only a single track along its right-of-way. That's one of the reasons Hollywood film sets had a special look to them—no one recognized the appliances.

Even GTE phones were different from the more common models from Bell.

During the Depression, with all the displaced people headed west, away from wasted land and a busted industrial economy, the power brokers in California started getting nervous, and as the flood continued, became frightened silly. What would happen if all those people discovered that the ranchers and labor contractors were in cahoots to drive the wages of all farm workers down by ensuring an oversupply? What then?

So a little money and a lot of political influence went looking for the weakest link in the moral chain. And it turned up at command levels in the Los Angeles Police Department.

Over the years, the LAPD has had more than its share of rogue chiefs. Even potential reformers were bent by the power that comes with running a police force that ranked in size as the fifth largest army in the world. In the thirties that power was brought to bear at California's borders.

Sheriff's departments worked with railroad bulls to keep newcomers from coming by riding the rods. They certainly accounted for their share of mayhem. But it was the LAPD that really overstepped every legal boundary. Squads numbering fifty heavily armed officers were sent to the state's borders *on every highway* with orders to turn back anyone with less than a hundred dollars to show. Which turned out to be almost everybody.

Using agricultural inspection stations, bridges, or anything at hand, these men established barriers to free travel, not only along the borders of Arizona and Nevada, but Oregon as well. Not that the other states minded at first—until refugees who were turned back became the other states' problem.

In the end, it took undercover federal marshals to break up what California newspapers called "the bum blockade." And even then, it did not stop. Cities and counties simply hired local toughs to man the barricades and to burn out the refugee camps whenever they could. The borders remained effectively closed and the final death count will never be known.

Today, as we sail down the highway, confident in our right to go wherever we please, it's worth a moment to reflect on the price paid for our freedom by thousands of plain people whose only crime was the crushing burden of survival in a broken land.

West of the Cajon Pass, Barstow and Victorville stand like sentinels in a region, where distances are so vast that life even along the main road is risky and difficult. Even the desert towns found on maps are not towns anymore. Most began life as section camps for the railroad, retaining their alphabetic names when the highway was built. Amboy, Essex, Fenner, and Goffs now barely exist, though if you say the names quickly they give the impression of an expensive law firm.

Undoubtedly, it was the sparse population of these towns and the surrounding desert that gave rise to a truly horrifying construction plan for the Route 66 corridor in this region. Picture this: some Atomic Energy Commission physicists are sitting around Washington back in the late 1950s. They're trying to come up with new ways to justify the enormous cost of nuclear power—and their own jobs—to the American public. Plus which, they have a bunch of surplus atomic bombs sitting around Albuquerque, taking up shelf space.

The Cold War was on, of course, and in the race for weapons superiority it was important to use up some of the old stuff that no one knew how to get rid of, especially the high-radiation bombs that could leave any detonation site uninhabitable for half a century or more.

An idea occurs to the physicists. Why not move mountains with them, like for a new highway or something? And what better place to try this out than on the Great Mojave Desert. Remember that these are *very* dirty bombs—and the AEC guys are not exactly right-brainers—the desert is nothing but dirt to them anyway. If it all goes sour, where's the harm?

Enter the California Department of Transportation: highway builders in a state where more goofy projects find the light of day than anywhere else on earth. High-level discussions are scheduled. A low-profile public-relations effort is begun. Trial balloons are sent up. And at last, a full proposal is presented. The Atomic Highway is nearing reality.

The joint plan calls for no fewer than twenty-two full-scale nuclear bombs to be planted along a two-mile stretch of intended roadway through the Bristol Mountains. The destructive power of these bombs will be 133 times greater than the force of the two atomic weapons dropped on Hiroshima and Nagasaki. The effect of these buried devices would be to vaporize the mountains in their path.

And where would all that vapor go? Why, right into the atmosphere, of course. The blast would produce a primary dust cloud reaching a minimum altitude of 12,000 feet, with a diameter of over seven miles from ground zero. Of course, the resulting bang will shorten the route by almost fifteen miles. Golly, who wouldn't want that?

Incomprehensibly, the plan goes forward and officials from the federal government, Santa Fe Railway, and Caltrans are busy deciding where to put the reviewing stand and VIP seating. There is no record of anyone giving thought to the consequences of the blast for people living in nearby communities. But the officials did have their reviewing-stand decorations all picked out.

Happily, the Russians saved our bacon by unexpectedly signing the 1963 Nuclear Test Ban Treaty. That agreement stopped a whole lot of insanity right in its tracks. But the image of all that radiation released by American scientists on the life in our own desert lingers, troublingly.

Hamish McGill—we'll call him that—paid his taxes, cherished his family, and never had a single brush with the law. At least not until the state of California told him that a new highway cutoff would cross his property. Even then he did his best to accommodate the highway men. They could put their highway here or there, just so long as it didn't separate his livestock from the only source of water.

Now, the truth is that civil servants often lose sight of what they're about. The words *civil* and *servant* lose all meaning when small-minded—some might say pea-brained—officials get puffed up with themselves. The highway men realigned their proposed roadway all right. The new alignment not only threatened the McGill family's livelihood, it would pass right through their house.

Hamish resisted. He slipped on his small, square spec-
tacles every night to study the law governing rights-
of-way in California. The highway men were wrong and
he cited chapter and verse to Sacramento. The highway
men reacted by having McGill's entire ranch condemned,
sending the sheriff out with an eviction order.

Hamish resisted again. So the sheriff swore that McGill
and his whole family had assaulted a duly sworn peace officer. He sent deputies out to arrest everyone on the property, including the family dog if they could find one.

Hamish resisted yet again, and after what passed for a
trial, he was sent off in leg-irons to do ten years' hard
time in a Northern California prison. An older immigrant
to this country, Hamish took separation from his family
very hard, but he kept his nose clean in prison where, being the only literate, bespectacled prisoner, he ran the library and earned his con-name, Four-Eyes.

By the time they let Hamish McGill out he was nearly
sixty years old, his wife had died, and his family had scattered. But Hamish was not one to get angry when he
could get even. He landed a job as a janitor with the same
state of California that had taken his land and ruined his
life. He kept his mouth shut and read every piece of paper
in every trash basket he emptied.

By 1932, Four-Eyes McGill knew where every piece of
livestock owned by the California Highway Commission
was kept, when they were moved, what they were fed. And
exactly how they were branded—with a stylized **C H C**.

$$\left.\right)-\left(\right.$$

A year later, Hamish McGill left his job, bought a
large truck, and set up shop on the high desert, just off
Route 66 near Adelanto. His first incursion behind the
Highway Commission's fencing netted him a very fine
team of mules, with which he graded several long, double-
ramp pits. These were located not far from remote graz-
ing lands and would hide his livestock truck from view,
even in daylight.

From then on, it was a piece of cake. McGill knew
horseflesh and could still spot a good side of beef. So he
kept up his unauthorized transfers of Highway Commis-

sion stock until his personal record of what the State of California owed him was balanced out—with interest added at 6 percent for the time he had served in prison.

As his livestock interests grew, Hamish steadily moved them over to a little spread off Route 66 in Arizona. There, the locals found him to be an honest and friendly neighbor, running a fine herd—under his own Four-Eyes brand.

On the original alignment of Highway 66 that wound through downtown L.A., the route passed right by a Southern California legend: Ptomaine Tommy's. There are several well-known burger shacks around town that echo the name of the old beanery, now long gone. But the original Ptomaine Tommy's was an institution unto itself.

Back in the late 1920s, Tommy's—nobody called it Ptomaine's—was a booming business. And though the Twenties roared a lot less in Los Angeles than in Chicago, the restaurant was a favorite after-hours hangout for West Coast gunsels, movie people, and the local literati. F. Scott Fitzgerald hurled his lunch in Tommy's regularly when he was in town working on a screenplay. No reflection on Tommy's food, however, for Fitzgerald was a champion drinker of everything in sight.

But what really pulled 'em into the joint was not Tommy's celebrity status, but the food. Stars and mobsters of that period shared one characteristic: they loved to indulge themselves at low cost. And Tommy's provided big portions at rock-bottom prices. In fact, low prices were what allowed Tommy's to survive and reach stardom on its own—thanks to the Great Depression.

Tommy's had always offered a version of chili con carne. But in true California fashion, it was only a burger topped with chili beans from a small ladle. Still, the customers liked it and double orders at 30¢ each were common. Then the Depression really kicked in. Even movie stars had little more to spend than drifters, and at Tommy's it paid to know the code.

In this case, the code was "chili beans, con-carne size." That meant the hamburger patty would be the same, but a larger ladle was used for the chili at no increase in price. Soon the item was simply listed on the menu as *chili size*. It only cost a dime back then, but you can still order its namesake all over the West. So if ever there is to be an official Route 66 dish, let it be the chili size.

Of all the intangibles associated with travel along Route 66, the image of Hollywood was once the most compelling. If you had a promise of work there, so much the better. If not, maybe you'd be discovered. Maybe right along Route 66, on Santa Monica Boulevard.

Sometimes it actually happened. Sometimes the studio machine scooped up a Margarita Carmen Cansino or a Norma Jean Mortenson and made them stars. But mostly Hollywood was, and is, a place where something terrific *could* happen. That was perhaps its greatest attraction to someone headed west.

In the heyday of Route 66, of course, Hollywood was far more present than it is now. Virtually all films were produced on the huge sound stages around town. But all that effort was also invisible. Almost no one got onto the lots who didn't work there and something like the Universal Tour was completely unthinkable. Hollywood was so totally self-absorbed that another city almost stole the name right out from under it.

For as it happens, most movies were made in Culver City, home of companies like Metro-Goldwyn-Mayer, derived from Ince and Sennett's first studio. As it also happens, Hollywood is really not a city at all. Most of it is part of Los Angeles; some is in unincorporated areas of the county. Knowing this, and having been rebuffed by studio officials in a 1937 attempt to gain recognition for themselves, the Culver City council went right for the jugular. With no public discussion, they passed a resolution that officially changed their city's name to Hollywood.

Well, Los Angeles practically had a cow, and the squabble went on for months as cross-town moguls tried to use the issue to settle old personal scores. Finally, the Selznick studio (later Desilu) worked out a compromise. City fathers from both sides got together at Grauman's Theater, a few blocks north of Route 66. There, alongside the stars' footprints in the forecourt, they ceremoniously buried a movie-prop hatchet.

The hatchet is still there and so is Hollywood.

Capitol Records, whose disc-and-stylus tower still dominates the skyline above Route 66 in Hollywood, was a success right from the beginning. And no one was more responsible for Capitol's early rise in the recording industry than Nat "King" Cole.

Nathanial Coles followed his sweetheart to L.A. in 1937. He was only nineteen but he had a knack for keyboard styling, and was soon pioneering a brand new sound in jazz with a drummerless combo of piano, rhythm guitar, and bass.

By the mid-1940s, the King Cole Trio had a string of solid hits. But in the winter of 1946, history swerved slightly to include a chance meeting that would bring new glitter to the Cole legend and guarantee legendary status for Route 66.

Nat was wowing an upscale crowd at the Trocadero on Sunset Boulevard. Along with Ciro's and the Mocambo, the Troc ranked as one of the most influential nightclubs in show biz. So if you made it at the Troc, the world was your oyster.

The King Cole Trio was making it, but the schedule was a killer: straight sets from early evening until two in the morning—close to eight hours each night. Several new records were also in the offing, but Nat had yet to find a good "B" side for one of the numbers to be recorded in March. It was already February. Time was short and not much new material was surfacing.

But it would. Oh boy, how it would! For a young Philadelphia songwriter was heading west in his green Buick convertible. Bobby Troup was a former Marine and an eager beaver, with a seventeen-week hit of his own, "Daddy," to recommend him. But it had been recorded five years earlier. Bobby needed something new, kicky, jivey. Something cool to audition on the West Coast. Route 66 gave it to him.

Only a day or two into the trip west, Bobby was already searching for a lyric that had a little sizzle. His wife, Cynthia, suggested that he write something about being on the road, about US 40. Bobby thought that was a good idea but he reminded her that they would soon be picking up Route 66.

"Get Your Kicks on Route 66," Cynthia said, with the unmistakable meter those words hold. Bobby thought it was terrific and began to work on the verse and a musical line. As Bobby was passing through Saint Louie and Joplin, Missouri, the tune was developing, but it was nowhere near completion by the time he hit L.A.

Road song or not, it was *show*time. Bobby was armed with a new swing-blues number to audition called "Baby, Baby All the Time"—and an enterprising Hollywood agent who knew the right people. He took Bobby to the Troc.

After the last set, the agent managed to fast-talk a fatigued Nat Cole into a five-minute listen. As chairs in the King Cole Room of the Troc were being stacked atop the tables, Bobby sat down at the piano, and in his nervousness, fell backwards off the stage.

There have been better openings to a crucial audition, but as Bobby ran through the sultry chording and lyrics of "Baby," the song connected. Nat was impressed and asked for more, catching Bobby completely off guard. So the young songwriter came back with the opening of his Route 66 tune. It was only a fragment, a few bars. It was also enough.

Nat knew the jump-blues beat would work. He'd already had success with that formula. Besides, Nat knew Route 66 a whole lot better than most—the roadside diners and sagebrush motels of that two-lane ribbon from Chicago—he'd driven it himself a dozen times.

A recording date was coming soon and this could be the side he'd been searching for. When could Bobby have it finished? Tomorrow? No. A week, then? Done.

Next day, barely unpacked, Bobby checked in at the recording studio just a few blocks off Route 66 in Hollywood. In a practice room, he spread out a US map above the piano keyboard, tracing the route as the litany of towns came back to him. Oklahoma City, Amarillo, Gallup, Flagstaff, eye-blink Winona—had to have a rhyme for Arizona—and on west to San Bernardino. Place names and the road-beat began to fall together, ending with a bit of jive-talk.

Nat introduced the song at the Troc as soon as the chord sheets were ready. A few weeks later, the Trio recorded several numbers and broke for lunch. The session had gone well and everyone felt that they were greasing it. In that mood, Nat and the Trio returned to cut "Route 66."

One of the most memorable road songs ever recorded was done in just one take. Everyone in the studio knew the performance was flawless and the cut was good.

But no one, especially not composer Bobby Troup, knew then how good the song truly was, or what an enduring hit it would become. Yet the tune stayed on the hit parade for two years, and thousands of westbound travelers used it as their only road map. The song and the highway became part of the national consciousness.

Bing Crosby would do it next, with the Andrews Sisters. And over the intervening years, Bobby's song would be recorded by performers as diverse as Mel Torme, Bob Wills, the Four Freshmen, Chuck Berry, the Rolling Stones, Van Morrison, Charles Brown, Manhattan Transfer, Michael Martin Murphey, Asleep at the Wheel, and Depeche Mode.

Even as Route 66 itself was being decertified as a US highway by transportation officials, the song rolled on. In succeeding generations, there will surely be more pressings of the classic. But it was done first, and certainly best, in Hollywood, just a stone's throw from the highway itself.

Santa Monica is nestled snugly between the well-manicured lawns of Pacific Palisades, and the freer lifestyles of Venice, making the city a culturally neutral terminus for old Route 66. Santa Monica was named, not for the saint herself, but for two blue pools of fresh water that reminded an early missionary of that good lady's tearful eyes.

In recent years, Saint Monica has become more generally known as the chief inventor of body guilt, but that reputation has little effect on the performers at Muscle

Beach to the south or the exclusive tanning salons just to the north.

As with many city-business stretches of old Route 66, those crossing Los Angeles and Santa Monica are not typ-ical of the roadside images we carry of the highway in more open places. Yet the stories are often just as good.

Anyone approaching the beach after nightfall, in the late 1930s, was treated to an entrancing sight. For just beyond Santa Monica Pier was one of the major attrac-tions—or eyesores, depending on your personal view-point—a full-on gambling ship. And the presence of that offshore beacon of sin, gloriously lighted by night, gave the locals fits. It was probably less a matter of moral out-rage than the fact that no one ashore was getting much of a cut. Ultimately, the squabble led to the Battle of Santa Monica Bay.

The *Rex*, strung fore and aft with lights totaling over a million candlepower, was the dreamboat of one Tony "The Admiral" Cornero. And it must be said right up front that Cornero was not your ordinary gangster. Tony found smuggling too rough and got out of that racket right after he'd made his first million. Thereafter, he concentrated on entertainment-style gambling, drawing some 13 million players—at a time when Las Vegas was still a wide spot on dusty desert highway.

Ultimately, the presence of the *Rex* and Cornero's prof-its became just too much for the supply-siders of the day. Restaurateurs were annoyed by Tony's free buffets; movie-studio heads felt he was muscling in on their en-tertainment business. They began howling about moral impropriety and Attorney General (later US Supreme Court Chief Justice) Earl Warren served notice on Cornero.

The notice was duly ignored, as were others, and in 1939 an unlikely assault force made up of state, county, and local cops headed for the *Rex* in a bobbing flotilla of water-taxis commandeered from the Santa Monica Pier.

Cornero was not unprepared. He had machine-gun emplacements on the ship's mastheads—in case any of his mob friends decided to pull a heist—but had given strict orders to his men not to fire on the lawmen.

The lawboats, commanded largely by officers who were themselves regulars at the ship's tables, knew the faces behind all the gunsights ranged above them. They also knew that the raid was a joke and began slipping close enough to the *Rex* to accept complimentary bottles of brandy from friendly crew members.

After nine hours of circling everyone except Earl Warren, who was trying ineffectually to direct his squadron by telephone from Sacramento, felt that justice had been sufficiently served. With raucous farewells that could be heard on shore, the assault force withdrew. Not a shot had been fired. Not a single lawman had stepped aboard Cornero's *Rex*. The Battle of Santa Monica Bay was over.

Hollywood executives, cut out of the action aboard ship, nonetheless got a piece of the Cornero pie. *Mr. Lucky*, a film starring Cary Grant in a gambling-ship story, was released in 1943. And a television series of the same name, loosely based on adventures aboard the *Rex*, aired in the late fifties, with a marvelous score by Henry Mancini. Both did well financially as the green of Hollywood envy changed to the shade of money.

And Cornero? Far from Route 66, in the Nevada Desert, he put together his biggest deal: the Stardust Hotel and Casino, among the first of the great draws on the Las Vegas strip. But with irony even Hollywood couldn't top, Cornero suffered a massive heart attack and died on a gambling table. He was down ten thousand bucks.

POSTSCRIPT

Traveling Route 66 is an intensely personal experience. But never more so than here at the ocean's edge. From my very first family trip west, Route 66 has always had some influence on my life. When I was quite young, staying in Los Angeles just a block off Route 66, I discovered some busy home-style neighborhood restaurants, each with its share of solitary regulars.

We all turned up at about the same time every evening and I sometimes shared tables with two great storytellers who became heroes of mine. One was Rod Serling, the other was Paul Brinegar. A native of Tucumcari, Brinegar attracted little attention in town, but returned years later starring as the crusty old trail cook, Wishbone, in the television series *Rawhide*.

Most of the show was shot near Tucumcari. It was an ideal location for a make-believe cattle drive and Paul had plenty of stories to share with a youngster back in L.A.— like which members of the cast couldn't ride a horse for squat; which were the biggest party animals; and which kept young-and-tenders scattered among Tucumcari's thousand motel rooms. All pretty juicy stuff.

Those stories are blurry now but I do have a clear

memory of a cast member Paul brought along to dinner one night. The young actor's in-your-face manner, coupled with a sandy voice that was both soothing and unnerving, made me agree with Paul that, from any distance, this guy was star material. In fact, I still have an old eight-by-ten glossy that he sent along later. The photograph is signed: Clint Eastwood.

The end of the road is also a reminder of the emotional distance Route 66 covers on its way from the Heartland to the West Coast. In the balmy morning air, a tan, silver-haired woman in her sixties strolls sweetly down Ocean Avenue in a beaded jeans jacket and well-tailored denim miniskirt. She has great legs and wears the outfit perfectly—bringing it to life as she walks by.

Two young men leaning against a red Alfa Romeo follow her every movement with their eyes. She acknowledges them with a smile and they resume their conversation. On the rear of their car is a bumper sticker. Without apology, the sticker reads: JACK NICHOLSON FOR GOVERNOR.

Ah, Southern California, where everything is still possible.

MORE ON
ROUTE 66

HIGHWAY MEMORABILIA

BOOKS

A Death on 66, by William Sanders. St. Martin's Press, 1994 [$20.95]. This is a crackerjack novel of suspense and, no, the publisher didn't pay me to say that. Several recent works have used the highway as a backdrop, but in a peripheral way. Will Sanders, a fine Native American writer, goes to the heart of the road's culture, knows the surviving sections of highway in eastern Oklahoma, and has written a first-rate mystery set there. It's a great scotch-and-fireplace read. So pick up a copy, or failing that, burden your library with requests.

Rising in the West by Dan Morgan. Alfred A. Knopf, 1992 [$25]. The Joad family in *Grapes of Wrath* captured America's hearts, mirroring our own dark fears and joys and small triumphs as they moved on to California. Now *Washington Post* writer Dan Morgan tracks a real Oklahoma family, spinning out the true story of migration, loss, redemption. The saga is splendidly told in narrative and personal recollection. A grand chronicle of one family's journey from Roosevelt's New Deal to the Reagan Revolution.

Route 66: The Mother Road, by Michael Wallis. St. Martin's Press, 1990 [$18.95 softcover, $35 hardbound]. Carefully researched, warmly written. Lots of color photography. The definitive work on the life and times of US 66.

Greetings from Gallup: Six Decades of Route 66, by Sally Noe. This 1991 collection of archival photos, available from the Gallup Convention & Visitors Bureau [$12.50], is like discovering history looking back at you. It's wonderful.

A Guide Book to Highway 66, by Jack D. Rittenhouse. Self-published, 1946. Now available in a facsimile edition from University of New Mexico Press [$7.95]. The granddaddy of all Route 66 books and as useful as it ever was. Want to know if the if the Palace Hotel in Winslow is a survivor from the old days on the highway? Jack's book can tell you.

MAPS

Return to Route 66, by Shellee Graham, Council Oak Books, 1998 [$9.95]. Sparkling, postcard-style collection of Shellee's photographs, including the remarkable "Dog on Route 66." Shellee's images are well known—her work has appeared on "Good Morning America"—and these postcards carry a hand-tinted quality not seen since the road was in its heyday. Order from your bookseller or Council Oak Books, 1350 E. 15th, Tulsa, OK 74120.

Bicycle Guide for Route 66, by Dan Mahnke, 1992 [$7.50 + $2.50 S&H]. Invaluable resource for bike-tour planning, with 102 pages of detailed mileage and elevations for riders, plus black-and-white photographs. Available from the author, 2791 University Avenue Riverside, CA 92507.

Official Map of Missouri & Kansas Route 66. Easy-to-follow map of a beautiful section of the highway that can sometimes be confusing. Even the ads on the map's border are a pleasure. How else would you know about the Choctaw Phone Company? Available for only $2.50 postpaid from Missouri Route 66 Association, P.C. Box 8117, St. Louis, MO 63156.

Historic Route 66 Tour Guide & Map, written and produced by David Kammer and Carolyn Kinsman for the City of Albuquerque, with support from the New Mexico Department of Tourism. A benchmark for all city guides. Clear, informative, with full-color graphics. Available at no cost from the Albuquerque Convention and Visitors Bureau. Call (800) 733-9918.

AUDIO/VIDEO

Route 66: The Mother Road, written and produced by Davia Nelson and Nikki Silva. National Public Radio, 1983. If there is a source point for the renewal of public interest in the highway, this recording is it. The five programs making up the 60-minute program are also a lesson in what fine media production is all about. This audio cassette blends history, music, and roadside conversations with a fresh innocence. Now a part of the road's history, it is available postpaid for $15 direct from The Kitchen Sisters, 132 Rivoli, San Francisco, CA 94117.

"(Get Your Kicks on) Route 66," by Bobby Troup. London-town Music, 1946. One thing is certain, Bobby Troup's song was responsible for creating the highway as much as Route 66 helped Bobby write the song. But have you any idea how many performers recorded the song for major labels? Here's a list to get you started.

Bobby Troup	Van Morrison
Nat King Cole / King Cole Trio	Cal Collins
	Mel Tormé
Rosemary Clooney	Depeche Mode
Bing Crosby / Andrews Sisters	Leon Rausch
	The Replacements
Bob Wills	Michael Martin Murphey
Perry Como	
George Maharis	Route 66 Band
Manhattan Transfer	Asleep at the Wheel
The Four Freshmen	Natalie Cole
Johnny Mathis	Grady Tate
Buddy Rich	Lamont Cranston Band
The Rolling Stones	
Charles Brown	Sammy Davis, Jr.
Paul Anka	Buckwheat Zydeco
Bob Dylan	Tom Petty & The Heartbreakers
Chuck Berry	

If that whets your collector's appetite, here's good news. If you're looking for the original Nat King Cole version, Collectors' Music Choice, north of the route in Illinois, has it. They also stock Nelson Riddle's hard-to-find theme from the *Route 66* television series. Other items for roadies from Glenn Miller and the Great Gildersleeve to Kinky Friedman. Order toll-free or request one of their great little catalogs at (800) 923-1122. They'll also help you locate other versions of "Route 66" or any song via their music-search line—(900) 737-6647. They're nice folks who love music.

Recapture even more of that two-lane feeling as you drive on through the darkness with old shows like *The Whistler* or *Mysterious Traveler* on your car's cassette player. If you've been raised on television you'll be surprised at the feeling of intimacy these old shows convey. And it's the next best thing to being there.

To receive a super old-time-radio catalog, call Radio Spirits at (800) 723-4648. They are a great resource with a huge inventory of comedy, mystery, and drama from the golden age of radio. And they are good folks to know.

Bagdad Café, produced by Percy and Elianor Adlon for Island Pictures. Movie released in 1988, now available from Virgin Vision on videocassette. Superb story told with great humor and compassion. If Dante Alighieri just could have lightened up a bit, he'd have loved this film. Next time you pass a video store, don't go home without it.

COLLECTIBLES

If you're looking for unique designs, top quality, and fair pricing, you can't do better than Route 66 Collectibles. Run by friendly folks born and raised along the highway, they specialize in T-shirts, pins, vinyl Route 66 shield decals, and unique items not found in shops everywhere. For a catalog sheet of their current offerings, write: Route 66 Collectibles, 619 S. Hacienda, Suite 2, Tempe, AZ 85281.

SHARE THE SPIRIT OF ROUTE 66

Beginning with two roadies operating entirely out of pocket, the US Route 66 Association first brought national attention to the plight and promise of the old highway.

Since 1983, the association has worked to keep travelers and the media informed about Route 66, its rich history, and the spirit of adventure to be found from Chicago to Los Angeles. And you can help keep the spirit alive.

If you'd like to join the US Route 66 Association, simply enclose a check for $22 with your request for membership, and mail to the address below. You will receive a Route 66 Cruiser's Kit, including:

- UPDATE SHEET FOR *TRAVELERS GUIDE* READERS
- MEMBERSHIP CERTIFICATE READY FOR FRAMIN
- FIVE-COLOR EMBROIDERED JACKET PATCH
- MATCHING DECAL FOR YOUR WINDSHIELD
- HIGHLIGHTS OF THE AMAZING ROUTE 66

New members also qualify for discounts on Rou
signs, plus other highway memorabilia. It's a
enjoy the road while showing your support fo
uing nonprofit effort to keep travelers up-to

U.S. ROUTE 66 ASSC
P.O. Drawer 5323 • Oxnard, C

ROUTE 66 ROAD SIGNS

No doubt about it. Route 66 highway markers are prized collectibles. So, in response to many requests from readers, here is a brief guide to the road signs of Route 66.

A design for the very first U.S. highway markers was released in the 1920s by the Bureau of Public Roads. Letters and numerals were heavily embossed on a 16-inch × 16-inch steel shield, as shown in the Kansas sign below. These were the best loved and are the most prized of all Route 66 markers.

Original Route 66 signs bring astronomical prices, however, and antiqued forgeries are offered for $1,500 and up. Beware! Other reproductions costing up to $100 are often cheaply made and not accurate.

So it was a pleasure to find a family-owned company with *original* stamping dies from the 1920s. Cost of one of their signs to readers is $55, plus $6 UPS shipping within the US, or $18 for delivery to Europe. MN and SD residents add tax. New members of the US Route 66 Association are entitled to an additional discount—see page 185.

e 1-800-383-3156 for credit-card orders. Or send a al check drawn on any US bank to: Gopher Sign y, 1310 Randolph Avenue, St. Paul, MN 55105-*ure to specify the order number for each sign* and al-*eks for* delivery.

LINOIS	#105 TEXAS
SSOURI	#106 NEW MEXICO
'SAS	#107 ARIZONA
HOMA	#108 CALIFORNIA

ROUTE 66 TELEVISION SHOW

Hundreds of roadies have inquired about *Route 66,* the television show that brought a whole generation to the old highway. And what a show it was!

Each Friday night, Tod (Martin Milner) and Buz (George Maharis) hit the road to adventure in their Corvette. With duffel bags snuggled down on the rear deck, the guys found danger around every curve and romance in every town. Never has a show so captured America's restless spirit.

For many years, only grainy, off-air dubs could be viewed. Now Columbia House has a 10-volume Collector's Edition of original *Route 66* episodes, each with 2 complete one-hour shows. Phone 1-800-262-2001 for information on the series or to place a credit-card order.

bia Pictures Television

Route 66 was an incredibly popular show, air 1960–64, with finely crafted scripts by Stirling plus Nelson Riddle's great road theme. Eve fast-action standards *Route* 66 holds up we that find high drama in the solitude of a t

Filmed entirely on location, the serie like Robert Alman and supporting Alda, *Bruce Dern,* Robert Duvall, Robert Redford——all happy to be

EXITS FOR ROUTE 66 ATTRACTIONS

Space does not permit a listing of the 365 interstate connections with Route 66, its towns, and attractions. But if you are driving the interstate and can sample only a few highlights, here are some exits to watch for along the way.

ILLINOIS—I-55

SHIRLEY—FUNKS GROVE	EXIT 154
MCLEAN—DIXIE TRUCKERS HOME	EXIT 145
LITCHFIELD—ARISTON CAFE	EXIT 145
MITCHELL—CHAIN OF ROCKS BRIDGE	EXIT 3

MISSOURI—I-44

PACIFIC—RED CEDAR INN	EXIT 261
STANTON—MERAMEC CAVERNS	EXIT 230
ROLLA—ROUTE 66 MOTORS	EXIT 195
HOOKER—DEVILS ELBOW	EXIT 169
LEBANON—MUNGER MOSS MOTEL	EXIT 130
CARTHAGE—GRAND AVENUE INN	EXIT 18

KANSAS—I-44

RIVERTON—GRAFFITI BRIDGE	EXIT 1
BAXTER SPRINGS—MURPHEY'S RESTAURANT	EXIT 1

OKLAHOMA—I-44/40

AFTON—BUFFALO RANCH	EXIT 302
CLAREMORE—WILL ROGERS MEMORIAL	EXIT 255
CATOOSA—BLUE WHALE	EXIT 241
CLINTON—ROUTE 66 MUSEUM	EXIT 65

TEXAS—I-40

SHAMROCK—U DROP INN	EXIT 163
MCLEAN—DEVIL'S ROPE MUSEUM	EXIT 143
AMARILLO—BIG TEXAN RESTAURANT	EXIT 75
CADILLAC RANCH—FIN CITY	EXIT 62
LANDERGIN—ROUTE 66 ANTIQUES	EXIT 28

NEW MEXICO—I-40

TUCUMCARI—BLUE SWALLOW MOTEL	EXIT 335
SANTA ROSA—CLUB CAFE	EXIT 275
ALBUQUERQUE—CENTRAL AVENUE	EXIT 167
MESITA—SCENIC LOOP	EXIT 117
GALLUP—EL RANCHO HOTEL	EXIT 26

ARIZONA—I-40

HOLBROOK—WIGWAM VILLAGE	EXIT 286
JACKRABBIT—TRADING POST	EXIT 269
WINSLOW—OLD TRAILS MUSEUM	EXIT 257
METEOR CRATER—MAJOR LEAGUE HOLE	EXIT 233
FLAGSTAFF—MUSEUM CLUB	EXIT 201
S—SCENIC LOOP	EXIT 178

CALIFORNIA—I-40/15

—EL RANCHO MOTEL	MAIN STREET EXIT
CUCAMONGA—VISITORS CENTER	VINEYARD EXIT
—AZTEC HOTEL	MYRTLE AVE. EXIT
A—PIER AND PARK	LINCOLN BLVD. EXIT

CHICAGO–LOS ANGELES MILEAGE TABLE

Wondering whether to keep going or stay put in the motel you found with the great neon and magic fingers? Here's a quick estimator. Cumulative mileage is given for both westbound and eastbound travelers. Distances from one point to another along old Route 66 appear in the center. Comparable interstate distances are shown in parentheses.

All mileages shown here are the result of averaging corrected odometer readings with distances given in AAA publications and official state DOT maps, so the values may not exactly match a map you are using. But for all sources taken as a whole, the resulting differences will be as small as possible.

Westbound Read Down From Start	Start	Eastbound Read Up From End
0	Chicago, IL	2278
	40 (42)	
40	Joliet, IL	2238
	59 (64)	
99	Pontiac, IL	2179
	36 (40)	
135	Bloomington, IL	2143
	31 (32)	
166	Lincoln, IL	2112
	31 (31)	
197	Springfield, IL	2081
	46 (44)	
243	Litchfield, IL	2035
	55 (44)	
298	St. Louis, MO	1980
	64 (60)	
362	Stanton, MO	1916
	48 (43)	
410	Rolla, MO	1868
	63 (58)	
473	Lebanon, MO	1805
	57 (51)	
530	Springfield, MO	1748
	72 (77)	
602	Joplin, MO	1676
	35 (24)	
637	Miami, OK	1641
	64 (55)	
701	Claremore, OK	1577
	28 (23)	
729	Tulsa, OK	1549
	52 (50)	
781	Stroud, OK	1497
	60 (52)	
841	Oklahoma City, OK	1437
	27 (26)	
868	El Reno, OK	1410
	52 (59)	
920	Clinton, OK	1358
	43 (40)	

963	Sayre, OK	1315
	31 (32)	
994	Shamrock, TX	1284
	31 (28)	
1025	Alanreed, TX	1253
	67 (64)	
1092	Amarillo, TX	1186
	47 (46)	
1139	Adrian, TX	1139
	65 (64)	
1204	Tucumcari, NM	1074
	64 (58)	
1268	Santa Rosa, NM	1010
	77 (58)	
1345	Moriarty, NM	933
	37 (34)	
1382	Albuquerque, NM	896
	74 (46)	
1456	Laguna, NM	822
	30 (31)	
1486	Grants, NM	792
	32 (30)	
1518	Thoreau, NM	760
	31 (33)	
1549	Gallup, NM	729
	49 (48)	
1598	Chambers, AZ	680
	50 (48)	
1648	Holbrook, AZ	630
	— (32)	
1680	Winslow, AZ	598
	— (46)	
1726	Winona, AZ	552
	17 (14)	
1743	Flagstaff, AZ	535
	40 (31)	
1783	Williams, AZ	495
	43 (45)	
1826	Seligman, AZ	452
	62 (—)	
1888	Hackberry, AZ	390
	27 (—)	
1915	Kingman, AZ	363
	28 (—)	
1943	Oatman, AZ	335
	43 (—)	
1984	Needles, CA	292
	74 (80)	
2060	Amboy, CA	218
	80 (79)	
2140	Barstow, CA	138
	36 (34)	
2176	Victorville, CA	102
	29 (26)	
2205	San Bernardino, CA	73
	56 (54)	
2261	Los Angeles, CA	17
	17 (13)	
2278	Santa Monica, CA	0

END

INDEX TO THE TRAVELER'S GUIDE